Krindlekrax

"Well," Corky said, "you know when you sometimes feel a rumbling in the ground under Lizard Street? And people tell you it's a Tube train going by beneath?"

"Yes," Ruskin said.

"Well, it's not a Tube train," Corky said. "It's the thing that lives in the sewers. It's the thing that comes up through the largest drain in the street. It comes up at night, when we're asleep, and cracks pavements with its gigantic tail, scorching bricks with its fiery breath and digging holes in roads with its sharp claws."

"What is it?" Ruskin asked, breathlessly.

"Krindlekrax," Corky replied.

Krindlekrax

PHILIP RIDLEY

Illustrated by
Mark Robertson

RED FOX

For my Grandmother, Cissie –
at the bottom of the stone steps
I'm calling still.

A Red Fox Book

Published by Random House Children's Books
20 Vauxhall Bridge Road, London SW1V 2SA

A division of Random House UK Ltd
London Melbourne Sydney Auckland
Johannesburg and agencies throughout the world

First published in 1991 by Jonathan Cape Ltd

Red Fox edition 1992

Text © Philip Ridley 1991
Illustrations © Mark Robertson 1991

18

The right of Philip Ridley and Mark Robertson to be
identified as the author and illustrator of this work
respectively have been asserted by them in accordance
with the Copyright, Designs and Patents Act, 1988

Printed and bound in Great Britain by
Cox & Wyman Ltd, Reading, Berkshire

RANDOM HOUSE UK Limited Reg. No. 954009

Papers used by Random House UK Limited
are natural, recyclable products made from wood grown in
sustainable forests. The manufacturing processes conform to
the environmental regulations of the country of origin

ISBN 0 09 997920 9

I

It was the day for choosing a hero.

All the week before, Ruskin Splinter's school – St George's – had been casting its end-of-year play and only the role of hero remained. Ruskin wanted to play this part more than anything. "I was born to be a hero," he had told his teacher, Mr Lace. "Don't you think so?"

"I'm not sure," Mr Lace had replied, sucking a pencil. "We'll decide next Monday."

And now it was the day for deciding.

As soon as Ruskin woke up he stared at the photographs of famous actors that were stuck on his walls (Ruskin wanted to be a famous actor when he grew up) and started rehearsing lines from the play.

"I am brave and wise and wonderful," Ruskin said, getting dressed and going to the bathroom to clean his teeth.

He looked at his reflection in the mirror above the sink.

"What a hero you are!" he said to himself, the toothpaste frothing in his mouth.

Ruskin was nine years old, extremely thin, with a bush of frizzy red hair. He wore black shorts that showed off his knobbly knees, black boots that made his feet look too big, a black T-shirt that made his arms look like twigs, and glasses with lenses so thick his eyes became the size of saucers.

When Ruskin had cleaned his teeth, he looked out of the bathroom window.

"Good morning, Lizard Street," he said in his squeaky whisper of a voice.

Ruskin always said good morning to the Street. He loved the dark brick of the houses, the cracked pavements, and the road with its bumps and holes.

At the other end of Lizard Street, Ruskin could see his school, St George's. The school had turrets and was surrounded by iron railings with spikes on top. The school was so old that Ruskin's Mum, Wendy, had gone there when she was a girl.

"One day," Ruskin said, "I'll be the hero of Lizard Street."

Ruskin washed his face and hands, then went downstairs to the kitchen. His Mum was sitting at the table – an electric toaster on one side of her, an electric kettle on the other – pouring endless cups of tea.

"Kiss," Wendy said when she saw Ruskin.

Ruskin kissed her cheek.

"Tea?" she asked.

"Yes, please," Ruskin replied.

"Toast?"

"Yes, please."

Every morning Wendy said "Kiss", followed by "Tea?" then "Toast?", and every morning Ruskin kissed his Mum's cheek and said "Yes, please" to both questions.

Ruskin's Mum was very small, extremely thin, with a bush of red, frizzy hair. She wore a short black skirt that showed off her knobbly knees, fluffy pink slippers that made her feet look too big, a sleeveless, black blouse that made her arms look like twigs, and glasses with lenses so thick her eyes became the size of saucers.

"It's another hot day," Wendy said, pouring Ruskin his tea. "We haven't had any rain for weeks now. I've never known a summer like it. Poor Mr Lace's window-boxes are withering away. It's so hot my glasses keep steaming up, polly-wolly-doodle-all-the-day."

Whenever Wendy got flustered, she said, "Polly-wolly-doodle-all-the-day". Once, for example, she had no bread to make toast, and really panicked. She ran round the house crying, "No toast with our tea, polly-wolly-doodle-all-the-day! What shall we do? Toastless tea, polly-wolly-doodle-all-the-day."

It was left to Ruskin to go to Mrs Walnut's shop and buy a loaf.

Since then, Ruskin's house has always been well stocked with bread (and teabags, because that's *another* thing Wendy can't live without). Most of the bread turns green and mouldy and has to be thrown away, but at least they are never without their buttery slices of toast and marmalade, or toast and baked beans, or toast and scrambled eggs (or poached eggs, or fried eggs).

Ruskin looked at his Mum as she prepared his breakfast.

"If you're so hot," Ruskin said, "you should take your slippers off."

Wendy looked at Ruskin, shocked.

"Take my slippers off!" she exclaimed, spreading marmalade on his toast. "Don't be silly. I wouldn't feel dressed without my slippers on. What if we had a visitor and I opened the door in my bare feet? They'd see my toenails and the soles of my feet. Oh, what a thought, Ruskin. It makes me say 'polly-wolly-doodle-all-the-day' just thinking of it."

"But we never have any visitors," Ruskin remarked. "No one ever knocks on our door."

Wendy put fresh slices of bread into the toaster. "What about Sparkey?" she asked.

"I'm not friends with Sparkey any more," Ruskin replied. "You know that."

"Oh, it's too early in the morning for arguments," Wendy said, sighing. "Just eat your toast."

Ruskin nibbled his toast, mumbling, "I am brave and wise and wonderful and handsome and tall and covered in muscles, with a voice like thunder . . ."

"Excuse me," Wendy interrupted, "but what's that you're twittering on about?"

"It's the hero's speech," Ruskin explained. "From the play we're doing at school. It's about this village that's gradually being destroyed by a dragon. The dragon lives in a cave and every night it comes out and digs up the pathways and burns the farmers' vegetables and cracks planks of wood. Until, one night, a boy tames the dragon by throwing a golden penny into its mouth." Ruskin was just about to add that the village in the story was supposed to have been on the same site as Lizard Street is now – that's why the street is called Lizard Street in the first place and why the pub at the end of the street is called The Dragon and the Golden Penny – but he didn't have a chance because his Mum interrupted again.

"And *you* want to play the *hero*?" she asked.

"That's right," Ruskin replied.

"Let me hear the speech again," she said.

Ruskin took a sip of tea, coughed to clear the crumbs of toast from his throat, then began, "I am brave and wise and wonderful and handsome and tall and covered in muscles, with a voice like thunder . . ."

"I don't want to interrupt again," Wendy said, interrupting again, "but can I just say something?"

"If you have to," Ruskin said, irritably.

"Well, I'm not sure you're perfectly suited for the part, dear."

"What do you mean?"

"Just listen to what you're saying," Wendy said, biting into her slice of toast. "I mean, I'm sure you are brave and wise and wonderful. But I'm not sure you can pass for the other things."

"Be specific, Mother!" Ruskin demanded.

"Specifically, then," Wendy said, "you are *not* handsome, you are *not* tall, you are *not* covered in muscles, and you have *not* got a voice like thunder. In fact, your voice is such a squeaky whisper that even *I* find it hard to hear you sometimes."

At that moment, Ruskin's Dad, Winston, came down for breakfast.

Wendy said, "Kiss."

Winston kissed her cheek.

"Tea?" Wendy asked.

"Yes, please," Winston responded, sighing.

"Toast?"

"Yes, please," he replied, sitting at the table.

Winston was small, extremely thin, with a bush of frizzy red hair. He wore pyjama bottoms with holes showing off his knobbly knees, woolly socks that made his feet look furry, a sleeveless vest that made his arms look like twigs, and glasses with lenses so thick his eyes appeared the size of saucers.

Wendy put some more bread in the toaster and poured Winston a cup of tea. Then she told him about the part Ruskin wanted in the school play.

"What does the hero look like?" Winston asked.

"Handsome," Wendy said.

"But Ruskin's not handsome," Winston said. "He's the silliest-looking boy in Lizard Street."

"And tall," Wendy said.

"But Ruskin's not tall," Winston said. "He's the smallest boy in Lizard Street."

"And covered in muscles."

"But Ruskin hasn't got any muscles anywhere," Winston said.

"And with a voice like thunder," Wendy said.

"But Ruskin's voice is just a squeaky whisper," Winston said. Then, looking at his son, he continued, "You can't possibly play the hero. People will laugh at you."

The toast popped out of the toaster. Wendy put some more bread in, then buttered the toast. There was so much toast piled up on the table now, that Ruskin had to stand on his chair to see his Mum and Dad behind it.

"But I want to be a hero," Ruskin said.

"We all might want to be heroes," Winston said, "but we're all not. You know my motto, 'Don't interfere'. Heroes have to do a lot of interfering."

"You know your trouble," Ruskin said, pointing at his Dad. "Low self-image!"

Suddenly there was a loud crash!

The kitchen window smashed and a football landed on the table, right in the middle of the toast.

Wendy screamed and hid behind the refrigerator.

Winston screamed and hid behind the gas cooker. "It's not my fault," he cried. "It's not my fault!"

Winston was always saying "It's not my fault." For example, a couple of days ago when Wendy complained about how hot it was, Winston said, "It's not my fault." And when Ruskin said he didn't have any school-friends, and when a light bulb fused, and when Wendy broke a cup, and when a car backfired, and when a dog started barking, to these and many other things, Winston's immediate and only response was, "It's not my fault."

Ruskin stood on the chair, staring at the ball. It looked like an ostrich egg in a nest of toast.

"Who said it was your fault?" Ruskin said to his Dad. "It's Elvis's ball again, that's all."

Winston said, "That's the third time Elvis has broken one of our kitchen windows."

"Not to mention all my ruined toast," Wendy said. Then she added, "Polly-wolly-doodle-all-the-day."

Most people on Lizard Street were afraid of Elvis Cave. He was very tall and very strong, and always wore the clothes of an American footballer: huge padded shoulders, tight trousers and shiny helmet with a visor. Also, his voice was so deep (for a nine-year-old boy) that sometimes, when he shouted, it made the teeth in Ruskin's head vibrate.

Elvis and Ruskin were in the same class at school. Once, when they were both as small as each other, they had been friends. There had been three of them in fact: Ruskin, Elvis and Sparkey Walnut. But then Elvis became tall and big and started scaring people. He stopped being friends with Ruskin. Sparkey, who was scared, followed Elvis, and Ruskin was left without a friend. Except for Corky, the school caretaker.

There was a knocking at the front door.

"It's not my fault," Winston said.

"Polly-wolly-doodle-all-the-day," Wendy said.

The knocking got louder.

"Give him his ball back," Winston said.

"But you shouldn't give it back to him," Ruskin said, stamping his foot. "Elvis is always breaking our windows and we can't afford new ones. Look! Most of our kitchen windows have been replaced with newspaper. And it's not just ours. It's everyone's on Lizard Street. And no one ever says anything or complains because Elvis is tall and strong and they're all afraid of him. He even breaks windows when he sleep-walks."

12

Elvis had been caught sleep-walking several times, bouncing his ball. The ball made a distinctive, liquid sound when it bounced that can only be described as "Da-boing!"

The knocking at the door grew louder.

Elvis called through the letterbox, "If you don't give me my ball back, I'll knock your door down, you silly bunch of Splinters!"

"It's not my fault," Winston said.

"Polly-wolly-doodle-all-the-day," Wendy said.

Ruskin picked the ball up, jumped off the chair and opened the street door.

Elvis stood on the doorstep, glaring down at Ruskin. Behind him stood Sparkey Walnut.

Sparkey was Ruskin's height, had a face full of freckles and always wore the clothes of an American baseball player.

"Give me my ball, you useless Splinter," Elvis growled.

Ruskin handed the ball back to him. Slices of thickly buttered toast were still stuck to it.

"You've made it all dirty," Elvis said. "Right, Sparkey?"

"Yes, sir," Sparkey said.

Sparkey responded with "Yes, sir" to everything Elvis said.

"Clean it," Elvis demanded, thrusting the ball into Ruskin's chest.

"Why should I clean it?" Ruskin asked. "It's your fault it's got our breakfast on it. You shouldn't have smashed it through our window. Besides, it was my ball in the first place. You stole it from me . . ."

Ruskin stopped speaking as Elvis grabbed his frizzy hair and picked him up. Elvis stared into Ruskin's eyes (or, rather, his thick-lensed glasses).

"What a thin, weak, ugly little Splinter you are,"
Elvis said. "Right, Sparkey?"

"Yes, sir," Sparkey said.

"Now," Elvis continued, "when I put you down,
I want you to pick every bit of toast from my –
repeat: MY! – football. Understand?"

It was very uncomfortable to be held by the hair,
so Ruskin said, "All right."

Elvis put him down.

Ruskin picked the toast from the football. "Good
little Splinter," Elvis said, taking the ball back.

Elvis walked away down Lizard Street, followed
by Sparkey.

"Da-boing . . . ! Da-boing . . . !" went the ball as Elvis bounced it.

Ruskin closed the door and went back to the kitchen.

"What nasty boys your old friends have turned into," Wendy said.

"It's only Elvis," Ruskin said. "Sparkey's just afraid of him." Then he looked round the kitchen and asked, "Where's Dad?"

"Gone back to our bedroom," Wendy replied. "He hid behind the gas cooker for a while, mumbling 'It's not my fault' over and over again, then sneaked upstairs in case there was any trouble. You know what he's like."

Wendy buttered a slice of toast and gave it to Ruskin.

"Take this up to him," she said. "He didn't have a chance to finish his breakfast."

"I'll be late for school . . ." began Ruskin.

"Oh, I don't ask you to do much," Wendy interrupted. "Just take it up. I've got all this mess to clear up. All I can see is toast and broken glass, polly-wolly-doodle-all-the-day."

2

Ruskin's Dad was in the bedroom, surrounded by model animals. Some of them were made of fluffy material, some plastic. There were all kinds of creatures: penguins, snakes, bats, elephants, lions, tigers, giraffes, bears, seals, dolphins. Every time Winston got fed up, he would go up to the bedroom and talk to them.

Ruskin put the slice of toast on the bedside cabinet and sat next to his Dad on the bed.

"How are the animals today?" Ruskin asked.

"Fine," Winston said.

"The fluff's coming off the penguins," Ruskin said.

"It's not my fault," Winston replied.

Years ago, before Ruskin was born, Winston had worked in a zoo. He wore a baggy, black uniform with brass buttons, and a cap that wouldn't fit over his frizzy hair. Winston had been very happy when he was a zoo-keeper. He loved all the animals and looked after them carefully. And then, one day, he got the sack and he didn't have a job any more.

Winston missed all the animals; their snorts and howls and grunts and barks, their feathers and fur and distinctive smells, the way they recognised him, nuzzling him with snouts or pecking him with beaks.

So Winston started to buy little toy animals to look after. He threw imaginary fish to the fluffy penguins, and imaginary steaks to the plastic lions and tigers.

"You didn't finish your breakfast," Ruskin said.

"It's not my fault," Winston said.

Ruskin asked, "Dad? Why did you get the sack from the zoo?"

"I've told you before," Winston said.

"No you haven't."

"Yes I have," insisted Winston. "And I don't want to talk about it any more. Now go to school and stop bothering me."

When Ruskin got downstairs he found his Mum kneeling by the front door, her nose pressed to the letterbox.

"What are you doing?" Ruskin asked.

"I can smell the drain," Wendy said. "First a smashed window, now this. Polly-wolly-doodle-all-the-day."

Just outside Ruskin's house was a huge drain. The cover to the drain was made of metal and it wobbled from side to side. Every time it wobbled it went "Ka-clunk".

In hot weather the smell from the sewer rose up and escaped through the wobbling drain-cover.

"Get up, Mum," Ruskin said. "I've got to go to school."

When Ruskin opened the door he found Dr

Flowers outside, standing on the drain and sniffing.

"Tishoo," Dr Flowers said.

Dr Flowers's nose was bright red and his eyes were watering. All summer long he sneezed and coughed and scratched his eyes.

His pockets were stuffed full of handkerchiefs and he pulled one out now as he stared at Ruskin and Wendy.

"Hayfever," Dr Flowers said, blowing his nose. "The only flowers on the street belong to ... TISHOO!" He sneezed again. "To Mr Lace." Dr Flowers looked over at Mr Lace's window-boxes full of marigolds. "And I can't ask him to ... TISHOO! To get rid of them. They're so ... TISHOO! Beautiful. TISHOO! TISHOO!"

Dr Flowers pulled another handkerchief from his pocket and blew his nose again.

"I see another one of your windows has been smashed by Elvis," Dr Flowers said, sniffing to ward off yet another sneeze.

"We haven't got many windows left," Wendy said.

"Mrs Walnut had her . . . TISHOO! Her shop window . . . TISHOO! Broken! TISHOO!"

"When?" Ruskin asked.

"Last night," Dr Flowers replied, rubbing his eyes. "Elvis was sleep-walking again. I heard the ball . . . TISHOO! Bouncing! TISHOO! But by the time I got into the street it was too late. The window had already been smashed. Poor . . . TISHOO! Poor Mrs Walnut."

"Oh, polly-wolly-doodle-all-the-day," Wendy remarked.

"Someone should stop Elvis," Ruskin said. "He's a menace."

"Who would dare stop him?" Dr Flowers asked. Then, "TISHOO!"

"I don't know," Ruskin replied. "Some hero, I suppose."

"Talking of heroes," Dr Flowers said, "I hear your school's choosing the hero for its . . . TISHOO! School play today."

"That's right," Ruskin said. "And I want to play the part."

"Well . . . TISHOO! You've got competition."

"Why?" Ruskin asked. "Who else wants the part?"

"Elvis Cave, of course," Dr Flowers answered. "TISHOO!"

3

Mr Lace – Ruskin's school-teacher – stood in front of the class and sucked his pencil.

Pencil-sucking was Mr Lace's favourite pastime. Sometimes he had up to five pencils in his mouth at once. Apart from his mouth, he had pencils in all his pockets, behind his ears, and even in his hair.

Mr Lace was tall and thin and always wore a scarf (even when it was summer) and a flower in his buttonhole (even when it was winter). His most striking feature, however, was not his pencil-sucking, or his scarf, or even his flower, but the way he sang his words when he spoke, as if singing along to music that no one else could hear.

Ruskin sat at the front of the class. Because he didn't have any friends, no one was sitting next to him.

The only other person to have a whole desk to himself was Elvis Cave. Elvis, however, sat alone because his padded shoulders left no room for anyone else. He spent all his time talking to

Sparkey Walnut (who sat at the desk behind), or bouncing his ball.

"Da-boing!" went the ball.

"Heroes, heroes, heroes," Mr Lace said (or sang). "What a problem heroes can be. Don't you think, class?"

"Yes, Mr Lace," the class replied.

Mr Lace ran his fingers through his hair. A few pencils fell to the floor. He picked one up and started to suck it.

"Who is to play our hero?" Mr Lace said. "That is our problem. And that's why we've got this . . ."

Mr Lace indicated something that had been at the front of the class since first thing that morning. No one knew what it was – because it was covered with white sheets – but it was very big.

"Can you guess what's under the sheets?" asked Mr Lace.

"A taxi cab?" someone suggested.

"No," Mr Lace replied.

"A speedboat?" someone else suggested.

"No, no, no," Mr Lace said, waving his hands in the air. "It has something to do with the play."

The class thought for a while.

"Is it alive or dead?" Sparkey asked.

"Well, it's dead now," Mr Lace replied. "But our imagination will bring it to life."

"A tree?" someone suggested.

"No," Mr Lace replied.

"A hill?"

"No."

"A hill alive with ants?"

Mr Lace was desperate now.

"No," he said, more pencils falling from his hair. "You can't be as silly as this. Think, class! Think!"

Ruskin had guessed what was under the sheets ages ago, but only spoke now.

"A dragon," Ruskin said in his squeaky whisper of a voice.

Mr Lace looked at him and smiled triumphantly.

"At last!" he exclaimed. "Of course."

And he pulled the sheets away, revealing a large, green dragon. It was made of paper and chicken-wire, with red milk-bottle tops for its eyes and cardboard egg cartons for the humps on its back. It had claws, sharp teeth, and a tail with a point at the end.

Ruskin shuffled with excitement.

"Right," Mr Lace said. "Now you can see what you'll have to confront in the play. Who wants to tame the dragon?"

For a moment no one moved.

"Come on," Mr Lace urged. "Who's our hero?"

Elvis put his hand up.

"Only Elvis?" Mr Lace asked, glancing at Ruskin.

Slowly, Ruskin put his hand up as well.

"All right," Mr Lace said. "We have two contenders. Ruskin Splinter and Elvis Cave. Ruskin, you can be first. Come up to the front and stand next to the dragon."

Ruskin's legs were shaking as he walked to the front of the class. The dragon was so big beside him. He felt insignificant in its shadow.

The class started to laugh.

"Shush now," Mr Lace said. "Give him a chance to say his lines."

But the laughing got louder.

"Shush, class," Mr Lace pleaded, waving his hands in the air. "Give Ruskin a chance."

But it was no good. The sight of Ruskin standing beside the dragon and wanting to be a hero was just too much for the class. Their laughter grew louder and louder and louder.

Some of them pointed at Ruskin and cried, "He's so small!"

Others cried, "He's so thin!"

Others cried, "His hair's all red and frizzy!"

"Shush, now," Mr Lace yelled. Then he looked at Ruskin and said, "You'd best sit down, Ruskin. I'm afraid the idea of you playing the hero is making the class laugh so much they might all burst a blood vessel."

Sadly and slowly, Ruskin walked back to his seat and sat down.

The class stopped laughing.

"Elvis," Mr Lace said. "Come up to the front of the class and stand beside the dragon."

Elvis stood up and bounced his football. "Da-boing! Da-boing!"

He walked up to the dragon and stuck his finger into one of its paper nostrils.

"I'm not afraid of you," Elvis said. "Silly dragon!"

The class started to clap and cheer. They clapped and cheered Elvis every bit as loudly as they had laughed and jeered at Ruskin.

"Very well," Mr Lace said. "Elvis will be our hero."

"Da-boing!" went the ball.

"Now then," Mr Lace said, looking at Elvis and sucking his pencil. "Are you sure you'll be able to learn all the lines?"

"Sure," Elvis said. "Easy."

I know all the words already, Ruskin thought. But he didn't say anything.

"You know," Elvis said, "I can't wait to be in a play. It'll make me feel like Shakespeare."

As soon as Elvis said, "Shakespeare", Mr Lace's eyes filled with tears.

"Oh, the wondrous Bard!" Mr Lace cried. "The joyous wordsmith who started it all."

"Sure," Elvis continued. "I really like . . ." and then he said the name as loudly as he could, ". . . SHAKESPEARE!"

"Oh, the Bard! The Bard!" Mr Lace cried, clutching his hair. "The magnificent master of all our imaginations."

Making Mr Lace cry at hearing Shakespeare's name was Elvis's favourite game. It had been Ruskin who had discovered Mr Lace's weakness, years ago, when Ruskin, Sparkey and Elvis had first gone to St George's School. But now Elvis was the only one who tormented the school-teacher in this way. He'd even given it a name: "Shakespearing Mr Lace."

"Oh, yes," persisted Elvis, bouncing the ball, "I've always admired . . . SHAKESPEARE!"

"The wizard of all beauty," wept Mr Lace.

The class started to laugh.

"Da-boing!" went the ball.

"SHAKESPEARE!" Elvis said.

"Oh, no, no, no, no!" Mr Lace cried, falling to his knees.

"SHAKESPEARE!" Elvis said.

"Oh, the wonderful Bard! The Saint of Stratford! The emotion wells up in me. Down my heart! Down! Down!"

Mr Lace was crying so much he could barely catch his breath. But Elvis still continued with the game.

"SHAKESPEARE!" Elvis said.

"Oh, the wondrous!" Mr Lace cried.

"SHAKESPEARE!"

"Oh, the Titan of all time."

"SHAKESPEARE!"

"Oh, the untouchable Maestro!"

Mr Lace was lying on the floor now.

"SHAKESPEARE! SHAKESPEARE! SHAKE-SPEARE!" shouted Elvis.

Every tooth in the class rattled at the sound of Elvis's thunderous voice.

Then the classroom door opened.

Corky Pigeon, the caretaker, stood there.

Corky was sixty years old, had grey hair and a wrinkled face and always wore a white overall. He also walked with the aid of a walking stick.

"What's going on here?" Corky asked in his gentle voice.

The class stopped laughing.

"Well?" Corky asked, walking up to Mr Lace and helping him to his feet.

"Nothing," Elvis said.

Corky glanced at Elvis.

"Have you been Shakespearing Mr Lace again?" Corky demanded.

"No," Elvis replied.

Mr Lace had stopped crying now. He dried his face with the end of his scarf and smiled at Corky.

"It was nothing," Mr Lace said. "It's my own silly fault for being such an emotional silly-billy when it comes to the name of . . . of . . . of the Bard."

"Well," Corky said, dubiously. "If you're sure."

Corky glanced at the class. He noticed Ruskin and gave him a wink.

Ruskin winked back.

Corky left the classroom.

"Thank you, Elvis," Mr Lace said. "You can sit down now."

Elvis walked back to his seat, bouncing the football all the way.

"Da-boing! Da-boing! Da-boing!"

"And tomorrow," Mr Lace said, sucking a pencil, "we'll start rehearsals."

4

"But I wanted to play the hero," Ruskin said.

"I know, my dear boy," Corky said.

"I'd make a good hero."

"I know you would."

School was over for the day and Ruskin was helping Corky Pigeon sweep the playground. Ruskin's broom was so large he could barely lift it.

The playground was made of asphalt that sparkled in the sunlight like crushed diamonds on black velvet.

Corky knew all about Ruskin wanting to play the hero, as he had been helping him learn the lines.

"*I* think you're a hero," Corky said, wiping sweat from his forehead.

"It's no good, Corky," Ruskin said, sighing. "When people look at me all they see are my glasses and frizzy hair and thin arms and how small I am."

"People are like that, my dear boy," Corky said,

27

sweeping some rubbish into a bin-bag.

After they'd cleaned the playground, Ruskin and Corky locked the iron gates and started to walk down Lizard Street.

Ruskin jumped over cracks in the pavement.

"Tell me," Corky said, tapping one of the cracks with his walking stick, "do you know what made the cracks?"

"No," Ruskin replied. "What?"

"Well," Corky began, "the cracks were caused by . . ."

Corky was interrupted by a voice exclaiming, "All sparkling and new!"

The voice belonged to Elvis's Dad, Mr Cave.

Mr Cave (along with Mrs Cave) owned The Dragon and the Golden Penny pub. He was a small, fat man who always had a cigar in his mouth.

At the moment of exclaiming, "All sparkling and new!" he was up a ladder and had just finished replacing a broken window. As he spoke, ash fell from his cigar and landed on Ruskin's head.

"Another broken window?" Corky asked.

"Elvis broke this one this morning," Mr Cave said, coming down the ladder. "He got Mrs Walnut's shop last night."

"I heard," Corky said. "You should take that ball away from your son."

"He means no harm," Mr Cave said.

Above them the pub sign swung in the summer breeze.

"Eeeek," went the sign.

"I must oil that sign," Mr Cave said, puffing his cigar.

The sign had a painting of a bright green creature on it. The creature was supposed to be a dragon and it had a golden penny in its mouth.

Mr Cave looked at the sign and said, "It's so hot the paint is peeling. If we get any rain now, it'll probably wash the sign away altogether."

A window opened above them and Mrs Cave poked her head out.

"Where's my Elvy-baby?" she asked.

Mrs Cave was small and fat and smoked cigars just like her husband. She always called Elvis her "Elvy-baby" and thought he was the best boy in the world. As Mrs Cave spoke, ash fell from her cigar and landed on Ruskin's head.

"He's out playing with Sparkey, Mrs Cave," Mr Cave said, ash falling from his cigar and landing on Ruskin's head.

"Elvy-baby!" Mrs Cave called, ash falling.

"Elvis!" Mr Cave called, ash falling.

Ruskin looked at Corky and said, "We'll have to go. My head's getting too ashy."

So they walked away from Mr and Mrs Cave.

Corky brushed the ash from Ruskin's hair.

Ruskin ran his fingers along the dark brick beside him.

"Tell me," Corky said, tapping one of the bricks with his walking stick, "do you know what made the bricks so dark?"

"No," Ruskin replied. "What?"

"Well," Corky began, "the bricks were made dark by . . ."

Corky was interrupted by a voice asking, "Do you want something?"

The voice belonged to Sparkey's Mum, Mrs Walnut, who was just about to close her grocer's shop. She was a small, thin woman with short, curly hair, who always smelt of potatoes.

"You're closing early today, Mrs Walnut," Corky remarked.

"I know," she said. "But I'm having to put in a new shop window. Didn't you hear? Elvis broke my old one with that ball while he was sleep-walking last night."

From down the street, Mrs Cave could be heard shouting, "Elvy-baby! Elvy-baby! Time for your tea!"

Mrs Walnut looked into her shop and called, "Elvis! Your Mum's calling!"

There was a pause. And then . . .

"Da-boing! Da-boing!"

Elvis Cave came out with Sparkey.

"I want an ice-lolly," Elvis said.

"You've had enough ice-lollies," Mrs Walnut said. "And besides, your Mum's got your tea ready."

"I always have an ice-lolly before tea," Elvis growled. "Don't I, Sparkey?"

"Yes, sir," Sparkey said.

"Oh, take one and go," Mrs Walnut said, sighing.

Elvis took a handful of ice-lollies from the shop freezer, then walked down Lizard Street towards the pub, closely followed by Sparkey.

"Sparkey used to be such a nice boy," Mrs Walnut said. "He's changed completely since Elvis grew so big. Why aren't you friends with Sparkey any more, Ruskin?"

"I want to be," Ruskin replied, "but Sparkey doesn't."

Corky said, "Actually, I do want something from your shop before you close, Mrs Walnut. I'll have a packet of chocolate biscuits."

Mrs Walnut went into the shop to get the biscuits. When she returned she handed them to Corky, saying, "I hope the chocolate hasn't melted. The sun's melting everything else. If we don't get some rain soon, the sun will melt the whole street away."

"I'm sure it will cool down soon," Corky said. "Nothing lasts for ever. It just lasts for little whiles at a time." Then he added, "Come on, Ruskin. Let's go and have our tea and biscuits."

As they walked down the road, Ruskin tripped over a bump in the road.

"Tell me," Corky said, tapping one of the bumps with his walking stick, "do you know what made those bumps and holes?"

"No," Ruskin replied. "What?"

"Well," Corky began, "the holes and bumps were made by . . ."

Corky was interrupted by a voice saying, "We've got a new film."

The voice belonged to Mr Flick.

Mr Flick was the manager of the Lizard Street cinema, known as the Dream Palace. He wore a black suit, with velvet lapels, black bow-tie and shiny leather shoes.

Mr Flick was just opening the cinema. Outside were photographs of the new film: men on horseback, holding shields and lances.

"Looks very exciting," Corky said. "Who wrote it?"

Mr Flick looked round – to make sure Mr Lace wasn't nearby – before replying, "Shakespeare."

"I love Shakespeare," Ruskin cried. "One day I'm going to be the greatest actor in the world. I'm going to stand on stage and do exciting things and the audience will watch me, holding their breath and biting their nails."

"You wanted to play the part of hero in the school play, didn't you?" asked Mr Flick.

"Yes," Ruskin replied, looking at the cracked pavement, "but I didn't get it."

"Who got it?" asked Mr Flick.

"Elvis," Ruskin said. "The class thought he looked more like a hero because he was tall and muscular."

"Oh, things like that don't matter to an actor," Mr Flick said. "I've seen some plays and thought the actors were as tall as a lamppost, but when I've seen them in real life, they've been shorter than me. It's what a person *does* that makes him tall, it has nothing to do with height or muscles."

Corky smiled and said, "Exactly, Mr Flick." Then he looked at Ruskin. "Come on, my dear boy. Time for our tea and biscuits."

"Can we see the film sometime?" asked Ruskin.

"Of course," Corky said. "It looks wonderful."

Corky lived next to the cinema. His home was small and dark and smelt of furniture polish and chocolate. Corky loved eating chocolate, especially the chocolate from chocolate biscuits.

Once they were inside, Corky put the kettle on. Ruskin sat at the table.

"The trouble is," Ruskin said, "I bet the whole of Lizard Street thinks Elvis will make a better hero than I would. I bet Mr and Mrs Cave think that, and Mrs Walnut, and Mr Lace, and Dr Flowers, even though Elvis breaks all their windows and they don't really like him."

Corky opened the chocolate biscuits and handed one to Ruskin.

"What does it matter what they think, my dear boy?" he said. "You know you could be a hero. That's all that matters."

"I know," Ruskin said, thoughtfully munching a biscuit. "But sometimes it's nice when other people think what you think."

The kettle boiled and Corky filled the teapot with hot water. He waited for it to brew, then poured two cups of tea and brought them to the table.

"I was called a hero once," Corky said.

"You?" Ruskin said. "When?"

"Oh, years ago, my dear boy," Corky replied. "When I was your age."

"What did you do?"

"It doesn't matter now," Corky said. "But I was given this."

Corky went over to a cupboard and opened a drawer. As he did so, his face glowed with a golden light as if the drawer contained a light bulb. Corky took something from the drawer, held it tightly in his fist, and the golden light disappeared.

He returned to the table and put something in Ruskin's hands.

The golden light returned.

It was a medal. A sparkling, gold medal.

"You really are a hero!" Ruskin exclaimed.

"That's what everyone told me, my dear boy," Corky said. "But I never felt like it. I mean, what does a medal mean? Nothing. To be quite honest, I feel more of a hero sweeping the school playground."

"In that case," Ruskin said, "I'm a hero as well. After all, I help you sweep the playground."

"Exactly, my dear boy," Corky said. "That's why I'm giving it to you."

"Giving me what?" Ruskin asked.

"The medal," Corky replied.

"Oh . . . but . . . you can't!" Ruskin exclaimed. "It belongs to you."

"If it belongs to me, I can do what I like with it. And I'd like to give it to you."

Ruskin stared at the medal. It was so bright and beautiful it made his eyes sting.

"And besides," Corky continued, "you deserve a medal for putting up with me. I'm so glad we're friends, my dear boy. I was lonely before I met you. Do you remember the first day we met?"

"I was seven years old," Ruskin said.

"That's right," Corky said, smiling. "Your first day at St George's. You walked in with Elvis Cave and Sparkey Walnut."

"We were all the same height then," Ruskin said. "All three of us were small and we were the best of friends. We did everything together. We'd ride our bikes and talk about insects and jump over cracks in the pavement. We saw you sweeping the school playground. We rushed up to you and asked your name."

"And I told you it was Corky Pigeon."

"Elvis asked if you were a teacher," Ruskin said.

"Me a teacher!" Corky said, chuckling to himself. "Can you imagine it? I don't even know the capital of Australia."

"And I started to talk to you," Ruskin said. "It was you who got me interested in acting. You told me about all the plays you'd seen and how some actors made you laugh and cry. And, one day, Mr Lace overheard us talking and you said . . ."

"Shakespeare!" interrupted Corky.

"That's right," Ruskin said. "You said, 'Shakespeare' and Mr Lace started to cry. That's when I discovered 'Shakespearing Mr Lace'."

"But you told Elvis," Corky said, frowning.

"He was my friend then," Ruskin said. "I trusted him. I thought I could tell him everything. But it all changed."

"Because he started to grow?"

"It seems that way. You gave me a football. Remember that, Corky?"

"Yes, my dear boy," Corky replied.

"It went 'Da-boing' when I bounced it. Elvis was really jealous. The next day, he just started to grow. He grew muscles, got bigger and started to wear those padded shoulders and a helmet."

"And he stole your ball."

"That's right. And Sparkey – who used to be my friend – stopped talking to me and started following Elvis around everywhere, saying 'Yes, sir' to everything Elvis said. And now I've got no friends. Except you, Corky."

"And I've got no friends, except you, Ruskin."

They hugged each other.

Corky's hair was very soft against Ruskin's cheek, like feathers, and Ruskin could feel the old man's heart beating through his clothes.

Suddenly Ruskin exclaimed, "But the cracks, Corky! The cracks and the dark brick and the holes and bumps in the road. You were going to tell me what caused them."

"So I was, my dear boy," Corky said, softly.

There was a pause.

"Go on, then," Ruskin urged.

Corky took a biscuit and started to lick the chocolate.

"It's quite a story," Corky said. "More strange than Elvis growing into the window-smasher of Lizard Street. It's a story so strange, you might not believe it."

"I'll believe it," Ruskin said. "Tell me."

"Well," Corky said, "you know when you sometimes feel a rumbling in the ground under Lizard Street? And people tell you it's a tube train going by beneath?"

"Yes," Ruskin said.

"Well, it's not a tube train," Corky said. "It's the thing that lives in the sewers. It's the thing that comes up through the largest drain in the street. It comes up at night, when we're asleep, and cracks pavements with its gigantic tail, scorching bricks with its fiery breath and digging hoies in roads with its sharp claws."

"What is it?" Ruskin asked, breathlessly.

"Krindlekrax," Corky replied.

5

Corky dunked a chocolate biscuit in his tea and licked it thoughtfully. He licked it until all the chocolate had gone, then threw the biscuit away and took another from the packet.

"What's Krindlekrax?" Ruskin asked.

"To tell the story properly," Corky said, "I'll have to go back ten years."

"Ten years!" Ruskin said. "That's before I was born."

"That's right," Corky said, wiping chocolate from his lips. "Ten years ago a lot of things were different."

"What things?"

"Well," Corky said, "the pavements weren't cracked, for one thing. And the brickwork wasn't dark and the road didn't have holes and bumps in."

"Because . . . because Krindlekrax wasn't around then?" suggested Ruskin.

"That's right," Corky said, taking another biscuit from the packet. "And I wasn't caretaker of St George's School."

"You weren't!" Ruskin said, amazed.

"Oh, I know what you think," Corky said, dunking the biscuit in his tea and starting to lick the chocolate. "You think I've always been a caretaker and I've always worn a white overall and had grey hair and walked with a walking stick. But that's not true. Ten years ago, my hair was black and I walked without a limp, and I didn't work at St George's School."

"So where did you work?" Ruskin asked, sipping his tea.

"In the sewers," Corky replied.

"The sewers!" Ruskin exclaimed, nearly dropping his cup.

"Yes, my dear boy. The sewers. Underground where all the dirty water is. In the smelly dark. At least, that's how most people think of it. But I never thought of it like that. For me it was beautiful. The walls are bright green and the water makes a gentle, trickling noise. There are chambers big as cathedrals, and waterfalls so high you can't see the top. And when you speak, your voice echoes round you a million times until your ears ring and you get giddy. It's another world down there and I loved everything about it. I felt like an explorer. Being down there was a true adventure for me, my dear boy."

"If it was dark," Ruskin said, "how did you see?"

"I'll show you," Corky replied.

Corky got up and went over to a wardrobe. He opened the door, removed something wrapped in newspaper, then returned to the table.

"What's that?" Ruskin asked.

"Open it and see," Corky said, handing it to him.

The newspaper was very old and had turned

yellow. It smelt of damp and dust.

Carefully, Ruskin peeled away the paper, like peeling an onion, and inside he found a tin helmet with a torch stuck on the front.

"I wonder if it still works," Corky said. And he reached over and flicked a switch on top of the torch.

The torch lit up.

Corky took the helmet from Ruskin and put it on.

The torch gleamed like a brilliant third eye.

"How do I look?" Corky asked.

"Wonderful," Ruskin said.

"That's how I looked in those days," Corky said, sighing. "I was younger and I was wonderful and I felt like an explorer in the underground world of green cathedrals and majestic waterfalls."

"So why did you leave?" Corky asked. "Why did you stop being an explorer and become a caretaker?"

"Because," Corky replied, "I was the one who found Krindlekrax."

Ruskin shivered so violently he nearly dropped his cup.

"Are you cold, my dear boy?" asked Corky.

"No. I just . . ."

"More tea?" asked Corky.

"No," Ruskin said.

"Are you ill?"

"Just finish your story!" cried Ruskin, in the closest his squeaky whisper of a voice could get to a shout. "Tell me about Krindlekrax!"

Corky took a deep breath.

"One day," Corky said, "I was underground when I heard a noise. A noise like I'd never heard before. A sort of crying sound. 'Eeeek' went the noise. I looked all round. My torch beam cut through the darkness. And there . . . there – on a ledge beside the trickling water – I saw something move. It was about the size of a shoe and bright green and had tiny sharp teeth. It was eating a slice of toast."

"What was it?" Ruskin asked, staring at Corky and clutching the edge of his seat.

"A baby crocodile, my dear boy," Corky replied.

"But how did it get there?"

"I never found that out. But there it was. Bright green and munching toast. There was marmalade on the toast and orange rind was stuck between the crocodile's teeth. There was something enticing about the tiny creature. I wanted to touch it. So I stepped forward. My feet went splash in the water and the light from my torch shone in the animal's eyes, making them bright red."

"Were you scared?" Ruskin asked.

"No, my dear boy. I just wanted to get closer to the crocodile, to feel its skin." Corky licked a chocolate biscuit for a while, then continued, "Slowly, I reached out . . . I could feel the crocodile's warm breath on my fingertips. And then, suddenly, the crocodile snapped its jaws shut. I managed to get my finger out of the way just in time. 'Clack!' went the jaws. Like two bits of metal clanging together. I took a step back, slipped and fell into the water. The water went up my nose and into my ears and made me cough and splutter. But I didn't have time to cough and splutter for long."

"Why, Corky?" Ruskin asked.

"Because the crocodile was already chasing after me," Corky replied. "I ran down the tunnel. The crocodile was very fast. I could hear its cracking jaws and the swish of its tail. I ran through the dirty water, hardly looking where I was going. I started to panic. For a moment I thought I was lost and would never find the ladder that led up to the surface again. 'Help!' I called. 'Help me, someone!'

"My voice echoed all round me. But no help came. No one could hear me. I was underground, my dear boy, and no living thing could hear me. Except . . ."

"The crocodile!" Ruskin interrupted.

"Exactly," Corky said. "Except the crocodile. But – suddenly – I saw the ladder. I grabbed it and started to climb. I was half-way up when I felt a terrible pain in my knee." Corky touched his leg, the one with the limp. "I looked down and saw the crocodile biting my knee. I shook my leg frantically. But the crocodile wouldn't let go. Its tiny jaws were clenched tight. Deeper and deeper its teeth went into my skin. I was yelling out. Finally, I hit the crocodile as hard as I could. It let go and fell back into the watery darkness. I heard it go splash."

Corky poured himself another cup of tea.

"Thirsty work," Corky remarked, "all this storytelling."

"So that's how you got your limp," Ruskin said.

"Exactly, my dear boy," Corky said. "I went to hospital and a doctor put a bandage round my knee and told me I'd be all right. But I wasn't! The crocodile had bitten through a tendon or something and I had to use a walking stick." Corky picked up the packet of biscuits and looked inside. "Only one left," he said. "Do you want it, my dear boy?"

"No, you can have it," Ruskin replied.

"You sure? I wouldn't want to cheat you of your share of the delicious chocolate."

"I'm sure, Corky. Just tell me the rest of the story. Is that why you left your job underground and became a caretaker instead?"

"Almost," Corky replied, licking the biscuit, "but not quite. I stopped going underground, but I still worked for the same firm. They gave me a job in an office instead. I stayed there for a couple of years. And then, one day, a worker went sick and they needed someone to go underground in his place to check a few leaks and rusty pipes."

"And you were the one who went," Ruskin said.

"That's right," Corky said, his tongue covered with chocolate. "I put my helmet on – this very helmet, with its torch – and went down into the darkness again."

"And ... and you saw the crocodile again?" suggested Ruskin.

"Oh, not at first," Corky said. "At first I didn't even think about it. I just concentrated on walking through the water without slipping over. And then ... and then I heard it."

"What?"

"A roar. A roar like I'd never heard before. Like a million car tyres screeching all at once. It made my bones shake."

"Were you scared?" Ruskin asked.

"Very."

"Because you knew what it was?"

"That's right, my dear boy," Corky said, licking the last of the chocolate from the biscuit and throwing it away. "I knew that for two years the baby crocodile had been drinking the dirty water and eating the remains of food. I knew that it had been growing and growing. And I knew something else. I knew that biting my knee had given it a taste for my blood. I knew that it had been growing and waiting for me to return so it could finish me off once and for all."

Ruskin leant forward and squeezed Corky's hand.

"What did you do?" Ruskin asked, eyes wide.

"Well, I didn't panic, my dear boy," Corky replied. "That's the worse thing to do. Never panic. So . . . slowly and calmly . . . I turned round and limped towards the ladder. I tried to be as quiet as possible. The splashing of my feet in the water sounded so loud to me. And then . . . then I heard it again. That terrible roar. I knew the crocodile was getting closer."

"Although it wasn't just a crocodile any more, was it, Corky?" Ruskin said. "It had got another name."

"It was Krindlekrax," Corky said. "I just knew that was its name. The roar of Krindlekrax filled my ears. I saw the ladder and reached out. I could hear splashing coming towards me. I knew Krindlekrax was getting closer and closer. I ran up the ladder. And, in those last few moments, I glanced down to see what was chasing after me."

"What did it look like?" Ruskin asked.

"Huge and dark," Corky replied, "with pointed claws and sharp teeth and breath as hot as fire. It was the most terrible thing I had ever seen." Corky leaned back and took his helmet off. "When I got home that evening," he said, "I saw that all my hair had turned white. The sight of Krindlekrax had drained the colour from me."

"So you left your job?" Ruskin said.

Corky nodded, saying, "Yes. I left, my dear boy. I got a job at St George's School. Where you and I became friends, so I can't complain too much."

Ruskin smiled.

"But I'll tell you something," Corky continued. "Some nights I know that Krindlekrax comes up through the largest drain in Lizard Street. I know it comes up and searches for me. And shall I tell you how I know?"

"How?" Ruskin asked.

"Because its heavy tail cracks the pavement, and its fiery breath scorches the bricks dark, and its claws put holes and bumps in the road. That's how I know."

"But . . . it's never . . . found you," Ruskin said, nervously.

"No," Corky replied, wrapping the old newspaper round the tin helmet. "And it never will."

"Oh, don't let it," Ruskin cried, getting to his feet and hugging Corky. "Don't let it get you. You're the only friend I've got."

"There, there, my dear boy," Corky said, holding Ruskin very tight. "Don't upset yourself. I'll never let Krindlekrax get me. I bolt all my doors and lock my windows and tuck myself in tight when I go to bed. I'm as safe as houses."

"If . . . if I ever see Krindlekrax," Ruskin said, "I'll tame him so you'll be safe for ever."

"None of us is safe for ever," Corky said. "We can only be safe for little whiles at a time."

Ruskin was still clutching Corky's golden medal in his hand.

"I'm still curious about this," Ruskin said. "Tell me why you got the medal."

"Not now," Corky said. "That's enough stories for one night."

"Is it anything to do with Krindlekrax?" Ruskin asked.

"No," Corky replied.

"Is it anything. . . ?" began Ruskin.

"It doesn't matter," interrupted Corky. "Now you get yourself home, my dear boy. Your Mum and Dad will be worried."

6

It was dark outside. Clutching the medal tightly, Ruskin walked down Lizard Street towards his home.

He looked at the cracks in the pavement and the holes in the road and the dark bricks, and imagined Krindlekrax walking up and down Lizard Street – its huge tail cracking, its sharp claws digging, its hot breath scorching – looking for Corky Pigeon. He imagined Krindlekrax looking in through windows, peeping through curtains, watching people sleep and dream. Perhaps Krindlekrax had even seen him – Ruskin Splinter – curled up in his bed, and wondered who this small, thin, red-haired boy was, sleeping contentedly in a room full of actors' photographs.

Ruskin stood on the large drain in front of his house. The metal drain-cover wobbled from side to side,

"Ka-clunk" went the drain-cover.

Ruskin thought, This is the largest drain in

Lizard Street. It's from this drain that Krindlekrax rises when he's searching for Corky.

Ruskin got to his knees and put his ear to the cold metal. He listened as hard as he could.

For a while he heard nothing. And then . . . then he heard it!

A distant rumbling.

The drain started to vibrate.

The rumbling got louder and louder.

So loud, Ruskin's knees started to tremble.

It was Krindlekrax! Down there in the sewer, it was stomping through endless corridors of water, through chambers as large as cathedrals and water-falls as high as mountains.

Ruskin got to his feet, brushed the dust from his knees, then looked up at his house. He noticed the window Elvis had smashed that morning had been covered with a sheet of newspaper. Nearly all of the windows were paper instead of glass now.

Ruskin went inside.

His Mum and Dad were sitting round the kitchen table, eating baked beans on toast. His Dad, Winston, was still in his pyjama bottoms and a white vest with holes in. The front of the vest was thick with baked bean and marmalade stains.

"Kiss," Wendy said

Ruskin kissed her cheek.

"Tea?" she asked.

"Yes, please," replied Ruskin.

"Beans on toast?"

"Yes, please."

Every evening, Wendy said "Kiss", followed by "Tea?" then "Beans on toast?" and, every evening, Ruskin kissed her cheek and replied "Yes, please" to both questions.

Ruskin sat at the table.

Winston's eyes were glued to the television set in the corner of the room. Someone on the screen was talking about the weather: "It's the hottest summer ever. Lawns are turning brown, flowers are drying up and we're running out of water . . ."

Ruskin said, "I wish we didn't have newspaper in our windows."

"We can't afford to keep replacing the windows," Winston said, still staring at the television. "Now the worst thing Elvis can do is rip paper instead of smashing glass."

"But it looks silly," Ruskin said.

"It's not my fault," Winston said.

"Oh, polly-wolly-doodle-all-the-day," Wendy said, handing Ruskin some tea and putting some bread in the toaster. "Don't make such a fuss."

"You should get Elvis's Dad to pay for it," Ruskin remarked. "Why don't you go and speak to him?"

"I don't want to speak to Elvis's Dad," Winston said. "Not now or ever! Besides, don't forget my motto, 'Don't interfere'."

Wendy poured Ruskin a cup of tea and asked, "Did you get the part of hero in the school play?"

"No," Ruskin replied.

"I said you wouldn't," Wendy said. "Fancy thinking a small, thin, red-haired boy like you with a squeaky whisper of a voice could pass for a handsome, tall, muscular, thunderous-voiced hero."

The toast popped out of the toaster. Wendy buttered it, poured some baked beans on top and handed it to Ruskin.

"We have toast with everything," Ruskin said.

"I love toast," Wendy said, ecstatically.

"But we can't eat all of it," Ruskin said, looking at his meal. "I mean, what happens to all the toast left over?"

"I throw it away," Wendy said, staring at the television set.

The person on the television was saying, ". . . paint is peeling, walls are cracking, people are getting sunstroke, drains are smelling . . ."

Ruskin asked, "Where do you throw all the toast?"

"Down the drain, of course," Wendy replied.

Ruskin looked at his Mum. The light from the television set reflected in her eyes, making them look like car headlights.

"Have you always thrown our uneaten toast down the drain?" he asked.

"Always," Wendy replied.

"The drain outside?"

"Of course," Wendy said. "After all, it's the biggest drain in Lizard Street.

Ruskin ate the rest of his meal in silence. Afterwards he went up to his room and sat by the window.

Now he knew why the baby crocodile had grown so big. Corky said that it had been eating toast when he first saw it. And that's what it had continued to do. For ten years. A daily diet of toast and butter, toast and marmalade, toast and baked beans, toast and poached egg (or scrambled egg or fried egg), toast and tinned spaghetti. And the toast had made the crocodile big and strong, had given it a tail and sharp claws and fiery breath, had transformed it from a tiny, bright-green baby, no bigger than a shoe, into a gigantic, dark monster that drained the colour from Corky's hair and nightly damaged Lizard Street.

"I'm going to sit here all night," Ruskin said, looking out of the window. "I'm going to stay awake and wait for Krindlekrax."

He stared down the length of Lizard Street. One by one the lights in windows (what windows were still unsmashed by Elvis's ball) went out and people went to bed.

Ruskin knew the street so well. He looked at Mr Lace's house with its window-box full of marigolds. He looked at Dr Flower's house, from where came the sound of the hay-fevered doctor sneezing in his sleep, "TISHOO! TISHOO! TISHOO!" He looked at Sparkey Walnut's house, where, no doubt, Mrs Walnut hoped her shop window would not be broken again by a sleep-walking Elvis. He looked at Corky's house where Corky was tucked up tightly, his windows locked, doors bolted, protecting himself from Krindlekrax. He looked at the pub, The Dragon and the Golden Penny, where Mr and Mrs Cave smoked endless cigars and Elvis lay in bed, his ball cradled in his arms. And he looked at the school at the other end of the street. The school, with its turrets and railings, was like a gigantic castle against the moonlit, star-filled sky.

Ruskin took the medal from his pocket.

There was a pin attached to the medal so it could be pinned on the owner. The medal gleamed in the moonlight.

The light reflected in Ruskin's eyes and made him feel tired.

Ruskin closed his eyes for a while . . .

He must have fallen asleep because, suddenly, he heard a noise and jumped up.

At first he thought it was Krindlekrax.

Then he realised it wasn't.

"Da-boing!" went the noise.

It was Elvis's football.

Ruskin peered down Lizard Street.

There – at the other end – Elvis was sleep-walking and bouncing the ball.

Even though Elvis was in his pyjamas, he still wore his American football helmet and the shoulders to his pyjamas were padded.

The moonlight made Elvis's shadow very long. It ran down the whole length of Lizard Street.

"Da-boing!" went the ball.

It was the only sound in Lizard Street and it echoed from building to building.

What a nasty boy you are, thought Ruskin, watching Elvis. You grow three times as big and steal my ball and you smash all our windows.

Suddenly, the ball struck a bump in the road and bounced off at an angle.

The ball hit Mr Lace's window.

"SMASH!" went the window.

One by one, the windows of Lizard Street lit up as people struggled out of bed.

The first on the street was Mr Lace.

Although he was wearing a long, white night-shirt, he still had his scarf round his neck and pencils in his hair. There was a pencil in his mouth as well, confirming the rumour that Mr Lace sucked a pencil in his sleep like babies suck a dummy.

"My window!" cried Mr Lace, waving his hands in the air.

Then he looked at the window-boxes. A few of the marigolds had been damaged by the ball.

"My flowers!" Mr Lace cried. "My beautiful flowers!"

Other people were in the street now.

Mr Flick in his jet-black dressing-gown with a velvet collar, Mrs Walnut in a pink, potato-smelling dressing-gown. Mr and Mrs Cave still smoking cigars, Dr Flowers with paper handkerchiefs stuck to his face. They all stood round Mr Lace and tried to comfort him as he bemoaned the state of his window-boxes.

"It's terrible," said Mr Flick.

"Outrageous," said Mrs Walnut.

"Disgraceful," said Dr Flowers. "TISHOO!"

"You're lucky," Mrs Walnut said. "He's broken my shop window six times now."

"And my window seven times," said Mr Flick. Ruskin's Mum and Dad were peering from behind their front door.

"He keeps breaking our windows too!" called Wendy.

"Shhh," said Winston closing the door. "Don't interfere!"

Mr Cave put his arms round Elvis and said, "Look how innocent he is. He doesn't even know what he's doing."

"My poor little Elvy-baby," said Mrs Cave.

Everyone in the street stared at Elvis.

"Now, then," Mr Cave said, "give him his ball back. Otherwise he'll be upset in the morning and you wouldn't want that to happen. You know how many windows Elvis smashes when he gets upset."

Mr Lace bit a pencil in half and went inside to get Elvis's ball.

"It's terrible," said Mr Flick.

53

"Outrageous!" said Mrs Walnut.

"Disgraceful," said Dr Flowers. "TISHOO!"

Mr Lace returned with the ball and gave it to Elvis.

As soon as it was in Elvis's hands, he started to bounce it. "Da-boing!"

Mr and Mrs Cave led Elvis back to the pub and locked the door.

The people of Lizard Street looked at each other in silence for a while. Then they shrugged their shoulders, sighed, and went to bed. All except Mr Lace, that is. He got a broom and started sweeping the broken glass.

Corky came out of his house and helped Mr Lace sweep the glass into a bin-bag.

"He's a nuisance, that boy," Mr Lace said, wiping tears from his eyes.

"Even in his sleep he scares us," said Corky.

Once all the glass was swept away, Mr Lace went into his house and locked the door.

Corky stood alone in the street for a while.

He glanced up and saw Ruskin sitting in his window.

Corky waved his stick in the air.

Ruskin waved back.

Corky went inside and locked his door.

Ruskin sat for a while, waiting for Krindlekrax. But, gradually, weariness overcame him and he knew he had to go to bed.

He changed into his pyjamas, looked at the golden medal, then closed the window.

"Goodnight, Lizard Street," he said.

7

The next morning, in school, rehearsals started on the play, *The Boy Hero*.

Elvis, holding a plastic sword and shield (and clutching his football under his arm) stood in front of the chicken-wire-and-cardboard-dragon.

Mr Lace watched from behind the piano.

"All right," Mr Lace said. "Begin your speech, Elvis."

Elvis took a deep breath.

"Oh, you terrible monster," Elvis began in a voice that, despite being loud and thunderous, was flat and emotionless. "You scary thing of . . . you scary thing of . . . the . . . the . . ." Elvis had forgotten his lines.

"Dark," prompted Mr Lace.

"Dark!" Elvis exclaimed. "You scary thing of the dark. You will scare us no . . . no . . . no . . ." Elvis had forgotten his lines again.

"No more!" Mr Lace prompted.

"No more!" Elvis exclaimed. "You will scare us

no more. I am not . . . not . . ."

"Afraid," Mr Lace prompted.

"Afraid!" Elvis exclaimed. "I am not afraid. I . . . I
. . ." Elvis's voice trailed into silence.

Mr Lace came out from behind the piano.

"Oh, well," he said to Elvis. "You'll be all right
once you've learnt the lines, I suppose."

Elvis put down his sword and shield and started
bouncing the ball. "Da-boing! Da-boing!"

"I'm going to be the best actor in the world,"
Elvis said.

"Yes," Mr Lace said, sucking a pencil. "The
whole class thinks that. Don't we class?"

Everyone in the class said, "Yes, Mr Lace."

Everyone except Ruskin, that is.

"Ruskin didn't say 'yes'," Elvis said.

Mr Lace looked at Ruskin.

"Oh, but I'm sure he meant to say 'yes'," Mr Lace
said. "Didn't you mean to say 'yes', Ruskin?"

"No," Ruskin replied. "I didn't."

"You didn't?" Mr Lace said.

"No," Ruskin said. "I think Elvis is the worst
actor I've ever seen. He's just saying the words, but
he's not feeling anything. I didn't believe a word of
it."

Silence.

Mr Lace stared at Ruskin.

Elvis bounced the ball. "Da-boing!"

"What's more," Ruskin continued. "He doesn't
know how to hold a shield and sword properly."

"Oh dear," Mr Lace said.

"Da-boing!"

"And he doesn't know how to breathe properly,"
Ruskin continued.

"Oh, dear," said Mr Lace.

Elvis was trembling with anger now. "Da-boing! Da-boing!"

"And he doesn't speak properly," Ruskin said.

The sound of the bouncing ball got louder and louder. "DA-BOING! DA-BOING!"

"And he shouldn't hold that ball under his arm when he's supposed to be acting," Ruskin said.

"DA-BOING!"

The ball bounced up to the ceiling, struck a light bulb, and went straight through a window.

"SMASH!" went the window.

Elvis pointed at Ruskin and growled. "You're not going to get away with that, you silly little Splinter. I'm going to smash your living-room windows, your bathroom windows, your hallway windows. I'm even going to smash the glass in your silly glasses. I'm going to smash so much glass around you, you're not going to be able to walk without crunching."

"Now, now," said Mr Lace, trying to calm Elvis down. "No need to get offensive."

"Oh, SHAKESPEARE!" Elvis snapped.

Tears came into Mr Lace's eyes.

"Oh, that wondrous name," Mr Lace said. "The Bard of all time."

"SHAKESPEARE!" said Elvis.

Mr Lace fell to his knees.

"Oh, the joy of the thought," he said, wiping tears from his eyes. "The fountains of emotion contained in that single name."

"SHAKESPEARE! SHAKESPEARE! SHAKE-SPEARE!" Elvis continued.

Mr Lace was lying on his back on the floor now, weeping so much his scarf became soggy with tears.

"I'm going to get my football now," Elvis said, suddenly tired of tormenting Mr Lace.

Elvis left the classroom.

After school, Ruskin helped Corky sweep up the broken glass from the school playground.

"Before long," Corky said, "Lizard Street won't be called Lizard Street any more. It'll be known as the Street of Broken Windows."

Ruskin told Corky how Elvis had threatened to break his glasses as well as all his windows.

"Are you scared, my boy?" Corky asked, sweeping the glass into a neat pile.

"A little bit," Ruskin replied, brushing the glass into a bin-bag.

"Well, there's nothing wrong with being scared," Corky said, picking up the bag. "We all get scared sometimes."

They took the bag over to a big, metal bin and threw it inside.

"Come on, my boy," Corky said. "Let's forget all about Elvis and his bad acting and his ball and his glass-smashing threats. Let's go and see the film at Mr Flick's Dream Palace. Would you like that?"

"Yes, please," Ruskin said.

"And we'll buy some biscuits on the way."

So they bought a packet of chocolate biscuits at Mrs Walnut's shop and went to the cinema.

They sat in the front row.

The cinema was dark and smelt of popcorn. The seats were covered with red velvet and there were bright orange curtains in front of the screen.

Corky opened the biscuits and offered one to Ruskin.

"I hope people don't talk during the film," Corky said. "I think that's a terrible thing to do."

The orange curtains parted and the screen exploded with light.

Ruskin tingled with excitement. He reached out for a biscuit.

The film was called *Henry V* and was in black and white. It was very exciting. Ruskin loved the charging horses and the "wooshing" sound the arrows made as they flew through the air.

Suddenly, Ruskin heard another noise. It was coming from the back of the cinema.

"Da-boing!" went the noise.

Ruskin looked behind him and saw Elvis Cave sitting next to Sparkey Walnut. The two of them were laughing and giggling and jeering at the film.

Elvis was bouncing his football.

"Shhhh," Ruskin said.

"Free country," Elvis said. "Can do what I like. Can't I, Sparkey?"

"Yes, sir," said Sparkey.

Corky turned round and waved his walking stick at Elvis and Sparkey.

"It's bad manners," Corky said.

"Da-boing!" was the only reply.

Ruskin and Corky faced the front again and tried to enjoy the film, but all they could hear was the relentless "Da-boing!" of Elvis's football.

Mr Flick walked down the aisle, holding a torch. The beam cut a neat white line through the dark, like an electric finger. He pointed it at Elvis.

"Please be quiet," Mr Flick said, straightening his bow-tie. "This is such a good film. Can't you hear the wonderful language?"

"It's not English," Elvis said. "I don't understand a word of it. It's all rubbish. Right, Sparkey?"

"Yes, sir," Sparkey said.

"But it *is* English," Mr Flick said. "It's the most wonderful English. It's by Shakespeare."

"Then Shakespeare can't write," Elvis said.

Mr Flick looked shocked.

"And it's boring," Elvis continued, standing up. He started to walk down the aisle towards the screen, bouncing the ball in front of him.

"Lots of silly actors in silly costumes and saying a silly lot of old twaddle," Elvis said.

"Da-boing! Da-boing!"

"Please. . .," Mr Flick said.

"Is this what you call good acting?" Elvis asked, looking at Ruskin. "Well, you're an idiot. I'm a better actor than all those silly idiots up there!"

And he bounced the ball as hard as he could.

The ball shot into the air and ripped through the screen.

A large, black hole appeared where the actor's head should have been.

Elvis screamed with laughter.

Sparkey screamed with laughter too.

Mr Flick just screamed.

Elvis and Sparkey ran out of the cinema, and Mr Flick stopped the film and turned the lights on.

"My poor screen," said Mr Flick, running his fingers up and down his black velvet lapels. "Now I won't be able to show any more films."

"Elvis's football is smashing everything in sight," Corky said. "Everyone in Lizard Street spends most of their time sweeping up broken glass. He's such a wild boy."

"Someone has got to do something," said Mr Flick. "It can't just go on like this. Elvis is terrorizing everyone – even his own Mum and Dad – and no one seems prepared to do anything."

Corky and Ruskin left Mr Flick's cinema and walked home.

It was late evening now and the sun was setting, turning the sky bright red and yellow, with a few glimmering stars visible.

"Corky," Ruskin said, "are the actors in that film still alive?"

"Some of them are," Corky replied, "and some of them aren't."

"I want to live for always," Ruskin said.

"No one lives for always," Corky said. "We just live for little whiles at a time."

Corky stopped outside his front door and watched Ruskin walk the rest of the way home. Ruskin stood on the metal drain in front of his house.

"Ka-clunk," went the drain.

Ruskin turned to wave at Corky.

A breeze blew down Lizard Street.

"Eeeek" went the pub sign.

Corky waved back.

'Ka-clunk," went the drain

Ruskin went indoors.

His Mum and Dad were eating toast and watching television.

"Kiss," said Wendy.

Ruskin kissed her cheek.

"Tea?" asked Wendy.

"Yes, please," replied Ruskin.

"Beans on toast?"

"Yes, please?"

Later, after Wendy and Ruskin had gone to bed, Winston sat up drinking cans of lager. He was still sitting up and staring at the television set when all the programmes had gone off and there was nothing on the screen but a grey fuzz.

Upstairs in his room, Ruskin – who had been reading – could hear the telly buzzing and fuzzing. He knew that his Dad had got drunk (as this happened quite often) so he went downstairs.

"Come on, Dad," said Ruskin, shaking Winston. "Time for bed."

Usually, this is all Ruskin had to do – shake his Dad, take the lager from his hand, and say, "Time for bed" – and Winston would obediently stand up, mutter "It's not my fault" a few times, and go up to his room.

But tonight was different – because, as Ruskin took the lager from his Dad's hand, Winston said, "The crocodile!"

Ruskin stared at his Dad.

Again Winston said, "The crocodile!"

Ruskin shook him.

"What crocodile, Dad?" asked Ruskin.

"The one I took," mumbled Winston.

"Took from where, Dad?"

"From the zoo."

Winston continued to talk in his drunken sleep.

And so it was that Ruskin learnt why his Dad had been sacked from his job as zoo-keeper and how the baby crocodile that bit Corky's knee and grew to become Krindlekrax got into the sewer in the first place . . .

8

Ten years ago, Winston went into The Dragon and the Golden Penny pub for a drink. He had just come home from work and was still wearing his uniform.

He went up to the bar, ordered a lemonade – the only drink he liked (at that time) – and sat by himself at a round, little table in the corner.

Winston had no friends in the street and always sat alone. In fact, most people thought he looked ridiculous in his baggy, black uniform and dusty peaked cap that wouldn't fit over his frizzy red hair.

Now and again, Winston tried to start talking to someone – especially Mr Cave, whom Winston desperately wanted to be friends with – but no one took him seriously and always referred to him as "silly Splinter".

That evening when he went to the pub most of Lizard Street was there: a younger Mr Lace (still wearing his scarf and sucking pencils), a younger Mrs Walnut (still running a grocer's shop and smelling of potatoes), a younger Dr Flowers (still covered in handkerchiefs and sneezing non-stop), a younger Mr Flick (still talking about films and wearing a suit with black velvet lapels and a bow-tie), and, of course, Mr and Mrs Cave (still short and fat and smoking cigars). The only people who weren't there were Wendy (who was at home), Corky (who was at work), and Ruskin, Elvis and Sparkey (who weren't born yet).

Dr Flowers was talking to Mrs Cave.

"You know," said Dr Flowers, "you really must get a . . . TISHOO! . . . a new sign painted for the pub . . . TISHOO! . . . The old one is all faded and ugly."

"That's what I've been saying," said Mrs Cave, puffing her cigar.

Mrs Cave was expecting a baby and was even larger than usual.

"Mr Cave," said Mrs Cave. "When are you going to buy a new pub sign?"

"I don't need to buy a new pub sign, Mrs Cave," said Mr Cave. "I'll paint one for myself."

"You can't paint for toffee," said Mrs Cave.

"Of course I can paint," said Mr Cave, puffing his cigar so much he almost disappeared in a cloud of smoke. "I can copy things, Mrs Cave."

"Well, in case you hadn't noticed," Mrs Cave said sarcastically, "you might be able to copy a few golden pennies but dragons are pretty thin on the ground these days."

"Don't be awkward, Mrs Cave," said Mr Cave, puffing his cigar.

"Don't be stupid, Mr Cave," said Mrs Cave, puffing her cigar.

The pub was so thick with the smoke from their cigars that everyone was coughing and spluttering.

Mr Lace opened a window to clear the smoke a little, and then said, "Why don't you choose something that bears some resemblance to a dragon and copy that?"

"Like what?" asked Mr Cave.

"Well," Mr Lace said, sucking his pencil thoughtfully, "like a crocodile."

"That's a good idea," said Mr Flick. "I've seen

films set a long time ago and the director has made crocodiles look like dinosaurs."

"But where would we get a crocodile from?" said Mrs Cave. "And, even if we could get one, wouldn't it be too big to get into the pub?"

Mr Flick frowned and thought.

Mr Lace frowned and thought.

Mrs Walnut frowned and thought.

Dr Flowers frowned and thought.

Mr and Mrs Cave frowned and thought.

For a while the pub was in silence, full of frowning and thinking.

And then a squeaky whisper of a voice said, "I can get you a crocodile."

The voice came from the small, red-haired zoo-keeper sitting by himself in the corner.

Everyone stared at Winston Splinter.

"You *can*?" Mr Cave said, picking some tobacco from his teeth.

"Oh, yes," Winston said. "I work at the zoo, you see. And there's a crocodile there. It's only a baby. Bright green and the size of a shoe. I could easily sneak it out for you. At least, I think I could. No. I'm *sure* I could. I'm positive I could. I'll put it in my pocket and you can have it for a whole night. Will that give you enough time to paint it for your sign?"

Mr Cave considered for a while, puffing his cigar. Finally, he replied, "Yes. I'm sure that's enough time."

"Good," Winston said, getting to his feet and walking to the bar. "Tomorrow night do you?"

"Perfect," Mr Cave said. "Let me get you a drink."

"Lemonade, please," Winston said.

That night Winston went home and kissed Wendy on the cheek.

"I think I've made a friend," he said.

The next day, going home after working at the zoo, Winston sneaked into the reptile house.

He walked past the snakes and the turtles and the salamanders, and went up to the glass tank containing the baby crocodile.

The crocodile was sitting on a piece of wood floating in water. It had pointed teeth and sharp claws and stared at Winston with bright, red eyes.

Winston took the lid off the glass tank and put his hand inside.

"Clack" went the crocodile's jaws, snapping at Winston's fingers.

Winston withdrew his hand. He was scared, but knew he had to get the crocodile, otherwise Mr Cave wouldn't be his friend.

He put his hand inside the tank for a second time.

"Clack-clack" went the crocodile's jaws.

Winston withdrew his hand again. He was so scared he was shaking.

"I know I'm scared," Winston said to himself. "But I've got to do scary things to get a friend."

So he took a deep breath and, whispering "Third time lucky", put his hand in the tank and grabbed the crocodile by its tail.

"Clack-clack-clack" went the crocodile's jaws.

Winston stared at the crocodile as it dangled from his fingertips. Gradually, the creature calmed down and stopped clacking its jaws.

Winston put the crocodile into his pocket and ran out of the zoo.

He went straight to the pub and gave the crocodile to Mr Cave.

"Be careful of its teeth," Winston said. "It's calm now, but it bites when it's angry."

Mr Cave took the crocodile and Winston upstairs to where Mrs Cave and Mrs Walnut sat on a sofa talking about what they'd call their impending babies.

Mr Cave put the crocodile on the coffee table.

"What a darling tail it's got," said Mrs Cave.

"What cute claws," said Mrs Walnut.

"And beautiful little teeth," said Mr Cave. Then added, "I'm going to start painting the new sign right away. I'll give the crocodile back to you first thing in the morning, Winston. Is that all right?"

"Fine," Winston replied, happy someone had called him by his first name.

That night, Winston was woken by the sound of a siren. He looked out of the window and saw an ambulance outside the pub. Mr Cave and Mrs Walnut were helping Mrs Cave into the back of the ambulance. Mrs Cave was wrapped in a blanket and kept saying, "I want a cigar. Get me a cigar."

The ambulance drove away (with Mr and Mrs Cave inside) and Mrs Walnut went back into the pub.

For a while, Winston thought nothing of it. He went back to bed and tried to sleep. Then, all of a sudden, he woke up and sat bolt upright, exclaiming, "My crocodile!"

Winston rushed out of the house and – still in his pyjamas – ran to the pub as fast as he could.

He knocked on the front door.

"Mrs Walnut!" cried Winston. "Mrs Walnut!"

He knocked again and again.

Finally, Mrs Walnut opened the door and asked, "What's wrong?"

"My crocodile, Mrs Walnut!" gasped Winston. "Is my crocodile safe?"

Mrs Walnut – who had been sleeping – looked surprised.

"Your . . . your what?" she asked.

"The crocodile I gave Mr Cave to copy for his pub sign," explained Winston. "The crocodile I took from the zoo. Is it safe?"

"Oh . . . goodness!" exclaimed Mrs Walnut, covering her face with her hands. "Mr Cave did paint the new sign. And then . . . then Mrs Cave went into hospital to have the baby and . . . Mr Cave went with her . . . and I was supposed to keep my eye on the crocodile but . . . I . . . oh, dear."

"You fell asleep!" cried Winston. "Let me in! Quick!"

They searched the pub, but the crocodile was nowhere to be seen.

All night Winston searched Lizard Street. He looked in rubbish bins, behind drainpipes, under cars, but the baby crocodile had disappeared.

In the morning, Wendy found him sitting on the metal drain outside their house. He was covered in dirt and his eyes were swollen with tears.

"The crocodile!" Winston said. "Where could it have gone?"

"Ka-clunk" went the drain.

At that moment Mr Cave walked into Lizard Street. He was smoking the biggest cigar anyone had ever seen.

"I HAVE A SON!" cried Mr Cave, giving cigars to everyone.

Mr Lace got a cigar.

Mr Flick got a cigar.

Mrs Walnut got a cigar.

Dr Flowers got a cigar.

Even Corky Pigeon (a younger Corky, with black hair and no walking stick) who was just leaving his home to go to work in the sewers, got a cigar.

Mr Cave shoved a cigar in Winston's mouth.

"I HAVE A SON!" Mr Cave cried again. "HIS NAME IS ELVIS!"

Winston got to his feet.

"Ka-clunk" went the drain.

Winston got dressed and went to the zoo. When he told them about the missing crocodile they instructed him to go and never come back. He would never be allowed to look after animals again.

Winston went home and put his uniform in a suitcase under his bed, then he sat at the kitchen table in his pyjama bottoms and a white vest and said, "I want some toast."

Wendy said, "Why don't you go out? I thought you said you had a friend."

"I was wrong," Winston said. "It's too dangerous having a friend. I shouldn't have interfered. I'm not going to interfere with anything from now on."

A few days later Wendy gave birth to a son.

"What shall we call him?" Wendy asked Winston.

"I don't mind," he replied.

"But you must have a preference?"

"I don't want to interfere," he said.

"Then I'll call him Ruskin," Wendy said.

After he'd finished telling his story, Winston fell asleep.

Ruskin stared at his Dad. He looked at the wrinkles round his eyes and the few grey hairs already appearing in his frizzy, red hair. He looked at the dirt beneath his Dad's fingernails and the holes in the white vest. He looked at how small his Dad was – how thin his arms were, how knobbly his knees – and, the more he looked, the harder he found it to believe that this man was responsible for Krindlekrax.

The ticking of the clock on the mantelpiece sounded very loud.

Ruskin glanced at the clock.

It was just gone midnight.

Way past Ruskin's bedtime.

Ruskin helped his Dad to his feet, took him upstairs and put him to bed.

Once Ruskin was in his own room, he looked out of the window down the length of Lizard Street.

He looked at Corky's house.

How could he talk to Corky again? How could he

be friends with Corky when his own Dad – Winston Splinter – had been responsible for Corky's white hair and limp.

At the end of the street the pub sign swung in the breeze.

Ruskin peered at the sign. Yes, now he could see. It wasn't a dragon with a penny in its mouth at all. It was a crocodile. A baby crocodile. The baby crocodile that had been taken from the zoo and escaped to the sewers.

"Eeeek" went the sign.

To Ruskin it sounded like the most terrible noise in the world.

9

The next morning, Winston couldn't remember a thing about what he'd said the night before. And Ruskin didn't tell him. All he said was that he'd found his Dad asleep and had put him to bed.

Wendy, Winston and Ruskin sat at the kitchen table eating their breakfast toast and drinking their breakfast tea.

"Polly-wolly-doodle-all-the-day," Wendy said. "I don't know how you can fall asleep in that chair."

"You say that every time," Winston said.

"Well, it's true," said Wendy. "All the legs are wobbly and it creaks when you move about."

Ruskin asked, "Why don't we get a new one, then?"

"Because we can't afford a new one," Winston said. "Why are you always wanting things?"

"I'm not always wanting things," Ruskin said.

"Yes you are," Winston persisted. "Give me this, give me that. It's not my fault I haven't got as much money as Elvis Cave's Mum and Dad. It's not my fault I haven't got a pub with a stained-wood bar and satin cushions and a carpet with magnolias on."

As Winston spoke, he sprayed Ruskin's face with bits of toast and marmalade.

"Calm down," Ruskin said.

"Don't tell me to calm down," Winston continued. "It's not my fault I can't afford to put new windows in and we have to stare at old newspaper instead."

A bit of toast went into Wendy's eye.

"Ouch!" went Wendy. Then she said, "Oh, polly-wolly-doodle-all-the-day, do shut up, Winston. Otherwise I'll have to have a bath to wash away all the bits of toast you're spraying everywhere."

But Winston just kept on talking.

"It's not my fault I have to wear these mouldy pyjama bottoms and a vest with holes in. It's not my fault I haven't got any friends and I watch telly all night. It's not my fault I haven't got a job and have to look after toy animals instead of real ones."

Bits of toast and marmalade were flying everywhere now. They stuck to the ceiling and stuck to the walls.

"My kitchen's a mess!" Wendy cried. "Stop moaning, otherwise everything will be covered with toast and marmalade."

But Winston wouldn't stop.

"It's not my fault we've got the biggest drain in front of our house and it goes 'Ka-clunk'. It's not my fault Elvis's ball goes 'Da-boing' and smashes everyone's windows. It's not my fault we live on a street with dark bricks and cracked pavements and a road that's got holes in it. It's not my fault I'm short and thin with frizzy hair and my voice is a squeaky whisper and I need glasses with lenses so thick my eyes look like saucers. It's not my fault! It's not! It's not! It's not!"

And with that, Winston went upstairs to stroke his fluffy animals.

Wendy looked round at the toast-and-marmalade-splattered kitchen.

"What a mess," Wendy said.

Ruskin got up.

"I'm going to school," he said.

"Why don't you go up and talk to your Dad?" Wendy said. "He's upset."

"I don't want to," Ruskin said, leaving the house.

As Ruskin walked down Lizard Street, he stared at Corky's house.

I'll never go there again, Ruskin thought. I can't face Corky now I know what my Dad did.

But, even as he thought that, he was already missing Corky's stories.

When Ruskin entered the school playground, he saw Corky mending the window that Elvis's ball had smashed the day before.

"Good morning, my dear boy," Corky said, waving.

But Ruskin didn't wave back. Instead he ran into his classroom.

That day, Mr Lace continued rehearsing *The Boy Hero*.

Elvis was still having trouble with his lines.

"You scary thing of . . . of . . .", Elvis said, then his voice trailed away.

"The dark!" prompted Mr Lace, from behind the piano.

"The dark!" Elvis exclaimed, holding his plastic sword a little higher and staring at the cardboard dragon. "You will scare us no more. I am not . . . not . . ." Elvis forgot his lines again.

"Afraid!" prompted Mr Lace.

"Afraid!" Elvis exclaimed. "I am not afraid. I have . . . have . . ."

"Tamed you now!" prompted Mr Lace, putting another pencil in his mouth (making three in all).

"Tamed you now and I am your . . . your . . ."

"Master!"

"Master!" said Elvis. But he was obviously fed up with the rehearsal because he had put down his sword and shield and had started bouncing his football.

"Da-boing! Da-boing!"

Mr Lace said, "Really, Elvis, you must learn your lines."

"Oh, I will," said Elvis, casually.

"I'm serious," said Mr Lace, sucking another pencil in his mouth (making four in all) and waving his hands in the air.

"When I've learnt my lines," Elvis said, "I'll be the best actor in the world." And he glared at Ruskin, waiting for him to contradict this.

But Ruskin had his mind on other things, so he just stared at Elvis in silence.

After school Ruskin rushed out of the classroom to avoid Elvis (who still wanted to "get him"), and ran across the playground to avoid Corky.

But Corky was at the main gate, already sweeping the playground, and it was impossible for Ruskin to get out without passing him.

"Hello, my dear boy," Corky said, putting his hand on Ruskin's shoulder. "Going to help me clean the playground?"

Ruskin stood still and stared at his feet.

"No," Ruskin said, softly.

"Oh!" Corky said. "Why not?"

"No reason."

"Have I done something to upset you?"

"No. Not you."

"Then who? Has Elvis been picking on you again?"

"It's not Elvis," Ruskin said, still staring at his feet.

"Look at me, my dear boy," Corky said.

Ruskin looked at Corky.

"Tell me what's wrong," Corky said.

"We can't be friends any more," Ruskin said.

"Why?" asked Corky.

"I . . . I . . . I can't tell you," Ruskin said. "Please don't make me."

Ruskin ran out of the playground and down Lizard Street as fast as he could.

"Ruskin!" Corky called after him. "Ruskin. Come back!"

But Ruskin didn't go back. He just kept on running; past Mr and Mrs Cave's pub, past Mrs Walnut's shop, past Mr Flick's cinema, past Mr Lace's house with its window-boxes full of marigolds and past Dr Flower's house where the doctor could be heard sneezing, "TISHOO! TISHOO! TISHOO!"

Ruskin sat on the kerb outside his house and buried his face in his hands. He could hear the drain go "Ka-clunk" and the pub sign go "Eeeek".

So now I've got no friends left at all, he thought. Once I had Sparkey and now Sparkey is gone. Once I had Corky and now Corky is gone. Perhaps that's the way it will always be. Perhaps we're not meant to have friends for ever, just for little whiles.

But what will I do without Corky? Ruskin continued thinking. No more talking to him about all the plays I've read. No more listening to his stories and watching him lick the chocolate from biscuits. No more helping him sweep the school playground and going to the cinema to see black-and-white films.

Ruskin was in the midst of his thoughts when he heard something right in front of him.

"Da-boing!" it went.

Ruskin jumped and looked up.

Elvis stood there, bouncing his ball. Behind Elvis was Sparkey Walnut.

"Not avoiding me, are you?" asked Elvis.

"No," Ruskin said.

"What?" said Elvis. "I can't hear you. Your voice is such a squeaky whisper the breeze just blows it away."

"I'm not avoiding you," Ruskin said, a little louder.

"You called me a bad actor," Elvis said. "And that annoyed me. Didn't it, Sparkey?"

"Yes, sir," said Sparkey.

"It's about time you found out once and for all," said Elvis, pointing at Ruskin with one hand and bouncing the ball with the other, "that I can do what I like. Right, Sparkey?"

"Yes, sir," said Sparkey.

"So you're going to get a scalp-scratching," said Elvis, grabbing Ruskin and holding him tightly. "What a muscleless, short, thin, squeaky-voiced Splinter you are."

And, with that, Elvis started to scratch Ruskin's

scalp, scratching him so hard and so fast that
Ruskin felt as if his hair was being pulled out by its
roots.

"Stop scratching me!" cried Ruskin.

"Can't hear you," said Elvis, scratching him
even harder.

"You're scalping me!" cried Ruskin, struggling
to get free.

"This should be a school game on sports day,"
Elvis said to Sparkey. "Scalp-scratching is such
fun."

"Yes, sir," said Sparkey.

Suddenly something fell from Ruskin's pocket and rolled into the gutter.

Elvis stopped scratching Ruskin and let him go. "What was that?" asked Elvis. "It looked like gold."

Ruskin held his sore head. He wobbled from side to side. And, although his head hurt so much he could barely think, he knew what had fallen from his pocket and what Elvis was about to pick up.

It was Corky's medal!

"It's mine," Ruskin said, faintly.

"Correction," said Elvis, clutching the medal in his fist. "It's mine. Right, Sparkey?"

"Yes, sir," said Sparkey.

Golden light reflected in Elvis's face as he stared at the medal. It glinted in his eyes and made him look quite mad.

"A medal," Elvis said. "I should have a medal. After all, I am a hero. Right, Sparkey?"

"Yes, sir," said Sparkey.

Ruskin made a grab for the medal. But all he managed to catch hold of was the pin.

"Go away!" said Elvis, pushing him.

The pin came away in Ruskin's hand.

"Come on, Sparkey," Elvis said. "Let's go and break some more windows."

And they walked away down Lizard Street.

Ruskin stared at the pin in his hands. That's all he had left of Corky's gift.

He put the pin in his pocket and went indoors.

His Mum and Dad were peering through a hole in one of the sheets of newspaper that replaced their window.

"You saw that," Ruskin said, angrily. "You saw Elvis scratch my scalp and steal something from me and you didn't do anything to help. You just watched."

"Best not to interfere," Winston said.

"Polly-wolly-doodle-all-the-day," Wendy said. Then added, "Kiss."

Ruskin sighed and sat down without kissing her.

"Tea?" she asked.

No answer.

"Poached egg on toast?"

Still no answer.

Wendy looked at Ruskin and asked, "What's wrong with you?"

"I just don't want to kiss you and I'm not hungry," he replied. "That's all."

"You're still upset about not getting that part you wanted in the school play," Winston said. "And, as I've said before, that's not my fault."

"It's not that," Ruskin said.

"Then what is it?" asked Wendy.

"I don't want to talk about it," Ruskin said. And rushed up to his room.

He lay on his bed, stared at the ceiling and thought about the first time he'd met Corky.

It was his first day at St George's School and he walked into the playground with his two best friends, Elvis and Sparkey. Corky was sweeping the playground.

The three boys rushed up to Corky.

"What's your name?" asked Ruskin.

"I'm Corky Pigeon," replied Corky.

"Are you a teacher?" asked Elvis.

"No," said Corky. "I'm a caretaker."

"What does a caretaker do?" asked Sparkey.

"I look after the school," Corky said. "I sweep the playground and mend the broken light bulbs and clean all the windows."

Elvis looked up at the school.

"There are a lot of windows," Elvis said. "It must take you ages to clean them."

"Oh, yes," Corky said, "It takes me ages, my dear boy. Sometimes I wish I never had to clean another window ever again."

And, from that day, Ruskin and Corky became good friends. They talked about plays and books and the dramas of Shakespeare.

Elvis asked Ruskin, "Why does Corky like you so much?"

"I don't know," Ruskin answered. "He just does."

"He doesn't like me," Elvis said. "But I don't care. I think he's a silly, white-haired old man."

Soon after that Corky gave Ruskin a football as a present, and Elvis started to grow and stole the ball, and everything changed.

Ruskin's thoughts of the past were interrupted by someone knocking at the street door. He heard his Mum answer it, then call up the stairs, "Ruskin! It's for you!"

No one ever called for Ruskin. At least, not since he had stopped being friends with Elvis and Sparkey.

Ruskin went to the top of the stairs and looked over the landing.

Corky was standing at the front door.

"Hello, my dear boy," he said.

"Hello," Ruskin said.

"Can I talk to you?" asked Corky.

A pause.

"Please," Corky said.

Ruskin went downstairs.

The two of them sat on the kerb outside.

"Ka-clunk" went the drain in front of them.

For a while they sat in silence.

Then Ruskin noticed that Corky was holding something. He looked closer and saw it was the metal helmet with the torch on it.

"What are you doing with that?" asked Ruskin. "Are you going into the darkness again?"

"No," replied Corky. "It's for you."

"But . . . but I don't deserve it," Ruskin said. "I ignored you when you called out to me and . . . Elvis has stolen the medal you gave me. All I've got left is a pin."

Corky smiled and shook his head.

"That doesn't matter, my dear boy," he said. "A pin is a useful thing to have."

"But . . . but there are other . . . things as . . . well . . ." stammered Ruskin.

"Listen," Corky said, "nothing matters, only that we remain friends. You understand me? That's the only important thing."

"So . . . you still want me for a friend?" Ruskin asked.

"I'll always want you for a friend," Corky said.

They hugged each other.

"Corky," said Ruskin, "I'm still curious about what you did to get the medal. Will you tell me the story?"

"Oh, I'm so tired," Corky said. "Can't it wait a while, my dear boy?"

"*Please*," pleaded Ruskin.

Corky sighed and said, "Well, I'll tell you as much as I can before tiredness overtakes me." Corky took a deep breath. "When I was a child – about your age – I had no friends. Don't ask me why. It's just the way it was. I think other children thought me strange because all I wanted to talk about were plays and actors and Shakespeare. So I played alone for most of the time. And my favourite place to play was . . . the dump."

"What's the dump?" asked Ruskin.

"Well, it's not there any more," said Corky. "But it used to be an area of waste ground. I used to play there every day. It was great fun. And then . . . and then . . . one day I found something . . ." Corky yawned.

"What was it?" asked Ruskin, eyes wide.

"At first, I couldn't make it out," said Corky. "It was sticking out of the ground. It was pointed and shining like the head of a gigantic silver fish . . ." Corky yawned again.

"Come on!" urged Ruskin.

"No, my dear boy," Corky said, rubbing his eyes. "Please forgive me, but I'm far too tired. I'll finish the story tomorrow."

"But . . ." began Ruskin.

"Tomorrow," said Corky.

Ruskin smiled and nodded.

"Now," said Corky. "Time for bed."

Corky stood up and walked down Lizard Street. His walking stick made harsh tap-tapping sounds on the cracked pavement.

When he got to his front door, Corky turned and waved to Ruskin.

"Ka-clunk" went the drain.

Ruskin waved back.

"Eeeek" went the pub sign.

Corky went into his house and closed the door.

Ruskin put the tin helmet on and switched on the torch. The beam of light shone all the way down Lizard Street.

Ruskin walked up to The Dragon and the Golden Penny. He shone the beam of light at the sign with the tiny green crocodile on it.

There it is, thought Ruskin. The baby that became Krindlekrax.

He stood at the sign for a long time, listening to it go "Eeeek" in the night-time breeze.

On his way home, he suddenly felt an overwhelming desire to knock on Corky's door, wake him up, and tell him he loved him. But he resisted. After all, it would be unfair to disturb Corky's dreams to tell him something he could be told in the morning. It could wait until tomorrow. Just like Corky finishing his story. Both things could wait.

Until tomorrow.

Ruskin walked home.

The noises of Lizard Street echoed round him.

"Ka-clunk!"

"Eeeek!"

"Da-boing!"

"TISHOO!"

IO

The next day, when Ruskin got up, he looked out of his bedroom window to say, "Good morning, Lizard Street" and saw an ambulance parked outside Corky's house.

Two men were putting a stretcher in the back of the ambulance. The stretcher had a white sheet over it.

For a moment Ruskin didn't move.

He just watched the ambulance and the two men with the stretcher and the people of Lizard Street standing nearby.

Mr Lace was there, wearing his scarf and sucking pencils.

Mrs Walnut was there, smelling of potatoes.

Dr Flowers was there, covered in handkerchiefs and sneezing noisily.

Mr Flick was there, in his suit with black velvet lapels and bow-tie.

Mr and Mrs Cave were there, smoking cigars.

Elvis was there, bouncing his ball.

Sparkey was there, saying "Yes, sir" to Elvis.

Everyone was there.

Except . . .

Ruskin saw something on the pavement next to the ambulance.

At first he thought it was a long twig.

But it wasn't a twig.

It was a stick.

A walking stick.

A walking stick like the one that belonged to Corky.

"Corky," said Ruskin, softly. Then louder, "Corky!"

He ran downstairs.

His Mum and Dad were peering round the front door.

"Something's happened to Corky," Ruskin cried.

"Don't interfere," said Winston.

"He needs me," Ruskin said, pushing past his Dad.

"It's not my fault," said Winston.

Ruskin ran down the street and up to the stretcher. He clutched at the white sheet.

"Don't, Ruskin," said Mrs Walnut. "There's nothing you can do."

"It happened early this morning," said Dr Flowers.

"We found him on the pavement," said Mr Cave.

"He was on his way to school," said Mr Lace.

"Must have been a heart attack," said Mrs Cave.

"Yes," they all murmured. "A heart attack."

The doors of the ambulance closed and it drove away.

The street was very quiet.

Ruskin picked up Corky's walking stick and stared at everyone.

He was trembling and his eyes were full of tears.

Ruskin knew it wasn't a heart attack.

He knew that – after all these years – Krindlekrax had finally got Corky.

"It's all your fault," Ruskin cried. "Every one of you." And he pointed at Dr Flowers, saying, "It's your fault because ten years ago you said the pub sign needed painting." Then he pointed at Mr Lace, saying, "And it's your fault because you suggested Mr Cave copy a crocodile!" Then he pointed at Mr Flick, saying, "And it's your fault because you agreed with Mr Lace." Then he pointed at Mr Cave, saying, "And it's your fault because my Dad wanted to be your friend." And he pointed at Mrs Cave, saying, "And it's your fault because you went into hospital to have Elvis!" And he pointed at Mrs Walnut, saying, "And it's your fault because you fell asleep and let the crocodile escape."

Ruskin ran back home. He pushed past his Mum and Dad and rushed up the stairs. At the top step, he turned round and pointed at his Mum. "And it's your fault because you threw toast down the drain." Then he pointed at his Dad, saying, "And it's your fault because you took the crocodile in the first place."

Ruskin ran into his room.

He flung open his window.

"I HATE YOU, LIZARD STREET!" he screamed, his voice louder than anyone had ever heard it before. "I HATE YOU! I HATE YOU! I HATE YOU!"

I I

Ruskin lay in bed. Spread out across the blankets in front of him were Corky's walking stick, the tin helmet with the torch, and the pin from the medal. Tears dripped constantly from Ruskin's eyes and soaked the pillows and mattress.

Wendy came up to see Ruskin.

"Kiss," she said.

"No," Ruskin said.

"Tea?"

"No."

"Toast?"

"No."

"Baked beans on toast?"

"No."

"Poached eggs on toast?"

"No."

"Scrambled egg on toast?"

"No."

"Fried egg on toast?"

"No."

"Then what do you want?" Wendy asked.

"I want Corky back," Ruskin replied.

Wendy sat beside Ruskin and stroked his forehead.

"He's not coming back, darling," she said. "You've got to understand that. He's dead. We've all got to die sometime. This is just the first time you've experienced it. Corky's body got tired, that's all."

"No," Ruskin said. "Krindlekrax got him."

"What's Krindlekrax?"

"The giant crocodile from the sewers. The one that Dad stole from the zoo. The one that cracks our pavement and scorches our bricks and digs up our roads. The one that's been searching for Corky for ten years. And now it's got him."

Wendy shook her head and said, "Oh, polly-wolly-doodle-all-the-day. Where do you get these stories from? You must get up. Everyone in Lizard Street is worried about you."

"I don't want to see anyone," Ruskin said. "Everything that is me hurts: my toenails hurt, my hair hurts, my eyelashes hurt, my teeth hurt. I feel tired all the time and I can't stop crying. There's an ugly taste in my mouth that I can't get rid of and when I fall asleep I dream that Corky is alive and the ambulance was a mistake."

"Have some tea," Wendy said. "Then you'll feel better. I've got some chocolate biscuits."

But the thought of chocolate biscuits reminded Ruskin of Corky, so he started to cry again.

"Corky can't be gone," Ruskin said, weeping. "How can he be gone when he didn't finish his story?"

Later, Winston came up to see him.

"Want a cup of tea, yet?" asked Winston.

"No."

"Toast?"

"No."

"Baked beans on toast?"

"No."

"Poached eggs on toast?"

"No."

"Scrambled eggs on toast?"

"No."

"Fried eggs on toast?"

"No."

"Then what do you want?" Winston asked.

"I want Corky back," Ruskin replied.

Winston left the bedroom and went downstairs.

Ruskin tried to sleep, but he kept on being woken up by the sound of Elvis's ball ("Da-boing!") and the squeaking of the pub sign ("Eeeek!") and the wobbling of the drain ("Ka-clunk!").

Lizard Street was continuing as normal.

But how could it? Ruskin thought. How could people continue as if nothing had happened? How could Mr Lace continue teaching and sucking his pencils? How could Mrs Walnut open her shop? How could Dr Flowers keep on being a doctor and sneezing? How could Mr Flick open the cinema and show *Henry V* on his new screen? How could Mr and Mrs Cave open the pub, serve drink, talk, smoke cigars? How could Elvis continue bouncing the ball, followed by Sparkey who continued to say "Yes, sir"? How could his Mum, Wendy, continue making tea and toast? How could his Dad still look after fluffy animals and say, "It's not my fault"? How could St George's School continue with its school play? How could everyone eat breakfast and dinner and watch television and go to bed and dream their dreams?

Ruskin imagined Corky's house, empty and collecting dust; a packet of chocolate biscuits uneaten, the seats unsat, the lights unlit, the carpets untrod. All those little things that Corky had collected throughout his life, all the things he knew, the things he'd seen, the plays, the films, the books he'd read, everything was gone, invisible now, as if they had never been.

Ruskin started to weep again.

"I wish I could stop crying," Ruskin said to himself, "but I can't. It's as if my whole body is full of tears."

The next day, Dr Flowers came to see Ruskin.

"TISHOO!" was the first thing Dr Flowers said. Then continued, "Now what are you doing in bed? It's been a week now. Seven days is too long to . . . TISHOO! . . . stay between the sheets."

Ruskin touched Corky's walking stick.

"I don't ever want to get up," Ruskin said. "I keep thinking of Corky and it upsets me too much to move."

Tears trickled from Ruskin's eyes.

Dr Flowers gave him a handkerchief to dry his eyes. Then he stared at him from the end of the bed.

"But you can't stay in bed for ever," Dr Flowers said. "Everyone in . . . TISHOO! . . . Lizard Street misses you and . . ." His voice trailed away and he started to sniff.

Ruskin thought he was trying to ward off another sneeze, but – instead – Dr Flowers said, "I can smell potatoes."

And, sure enough, the next second Mrs Walnut came into Ruskin's bedroom, holding a packet of chocolate biscuits.

"These are for you," she said, giving the biscuits to Ruskin.

"I can't look at biscuits without wanting to cry," Ruskin said. "They remind me of the way Corky used to lick the chocolate off them."

"But they're a present," Mrs Walnut said. "You can't refuse my present. Corky wouldn't have wanted that." Then Mrs Walnut started to sniff. "I can smell cigar smoke," she said.

And, sure enough, the next second Mr and Mrs Cave came into Ruskin's bedroom, with a bottle of cherryade.

"This is for you," said Mrs Cave, giving the bottle to Ruskin.

But Ruskin was still crying and wished they would all go away and leave him alone.

"My bedroom's getting too crowded," he said. "It's only meant for me. Not everyone in Lizard Street."

But still more people visited with presents.

Mr Lace came with some coloured pencils.

Mr Flick came with a photograph of the actor playing Henry V.

They all stood at the end of Ruskin's bed and stared down at him. The room was so hot and stuffy with their breath that the windows started to mist up.

"Get out of bed," said Mr Lace.

"We miss you in Lizard Street," said Mrs Walnut.

"I miss your squeaky whisper of a voice," said Mr Lace.

"I miss your knobbly knees," said Mr Flick.

"We miss your fuzzy red hair," said Mr Cave. "Don't we, Mrs Cave?"

"Yes," said Mrs Cave. "We do, Mr Cave."

And then, all together, they asked, "Why don't you get up?"

"BECAUSE I MISS CORKY!" cried Ruskin.

They all looked at him in silence for a while.

"Does anyone remember that story about Corky?" Mr Lace said, looking round the room. "About what he did when he was a child. Something about a medal."

"Oh, yes," said Mrs Walnut. "It was before our time. Years ago, I think. Corky was a boy. He was playing on a dump . . . a dump at the end of the street. Where the pub is now."

"That's right," said Mr Cave. "It was before the pub was built. There was nothing there but rubbish and rubble. Corky was playing on the site when suddenly he found something."

Ruskin had stopped crying now. He sat up in bed and looked at Mr Cave.

"What did he find?" asked Ruskin.

"Something sticking out of the ground," Mr Cave replied. "Pointed it was, and silver and very, very smooth. Made of metal."

Ruskin leaned forward.

"Like a giant, silver fish head?" asked Ruskin.

Mrs Cave continued the story.

"That's right," she said, puffing her cigar and flicking ash on to the end of the bed. "It was something from the war and very dangerous."

"A bomb?" Ruskin said.

"A bomb it was," said Dr Flowers. "Only Corky didn't know it was a . . . TISHOO! . . . bomb at the time, so he jumped on it and . . . TISHOO! . . . and it started ticking."

Ruskin gasped.

"But that means," Ruskin said, breathlessly, "if Corky was to move the bomb would have exploded."

"Precisely," said Mr Flick, continuing the story. "Luckily someone heard the ticking and yelled to Corky to keep still."

"So Corky kept still?" Ruskin said.

"He kept very still," said Mr Lace, sucking a pencil.

"He kept the stillest he'd ever been," said Mrs Walnut, her potato smell getting stronger.

"He kept still for hours and hours," said Dr Flowers, pinching his nose to ward off another sneeze.

"He kept still until some experts came and defused the bomb," said Mr Cave, puffing his cigar. "Didn't he, Mrs Cave?"

"He did, Mr Cave," said Mrs Cave, puffing her cigar.

Ruskin was so engrossed with the story that he pushed the covers off him and stood up on his bed.

"So that's why he got a medal!" cried Ruskin, bouncing up and down on his mattress.

Later, after everyone had gone, Ruskin lay in bed and thought about the story.

Corky had saved Lizard Street. He had saved Lizard Street all by himself. He was a hero.

And now it was Ruskin's turn. Now he had to protect Lizard Street too. Protect it from the thing that cracked the pavement, scorched the brickwork and dug holes in the road.

Ruskin knew what he had to do. That night, while Lizard Street slept, he would tame Krindle-krax.

12

Darkness.

Darkness and silence.

Night-time on Lizard Street.

Ruskin got out of bed and put his ear to the wall. He could hear his Mum and Dad snoring and mumbling in their sleep.

"It's not my fault!" his Dad was saying.

"Polly-wolly-doodle-all-the-day," his Mum was saying.

Ruskin got dressed, then put on the tin helmet and turned the torch on. The beam of light shot through the gloom and illuminated the photographs of actors on the wall opposite.

Ruskin picked up the pin that had been on the medal and put it in his pocket. Then he picked up the walking stick, waving it in the air like a sword.

"Now, unto the breach," Ruskin said, looking at himself in the mirror.

His red, frizzy hair stood out beneath the helmet and his arms and legs weren't much thicker than the walking stick.

Perhaps I don't look like a hero, Ruskin thought. But only I can save Lizard Street from the cracking and scorching and digging of Krindlekrax.

And, with that, he crept downstairs and went into the kitchen. The kitchen table was covered with piles of toast.

As quietly as he could, Ruskin picked up some toast, opened the street door and went out into Lizard Street.

The moon was full, illuminating the street with a ghostly blue light. The sky was clear and gleaming with stars.

Ruskin went up to the metal drain and started to lay a trail of toast, leading away from the drain and down the street towards the school.

He had to make several journeys back to his home because, at the end of the line, he wanted a pile of toast, to act as bait for Kindlekrax.

Just as he was picking up the last remaining slices of toast from the table, Ruskin heard something flapping.

He grabbed the walking stick tightly.

A bird, Ruskin thought. A bird is in the room.

He looked round the kitchen.

And, wherever he looked, the torch beam shone. It illuminated the toaster and the gas oven and the refrigerator and the dirty washing-up in the sink.

But it didn't illuminate a bird.

Then Ruskin realised what the sound was.

A gentle breeze was blowing outside, making the newspaper in the kitchen windows flap in and out, like something breathing, or a flapping bird's wing.

Ruskin heaved a sigh of relief and chuckled.

What a silly boy I am, he thought.

He went back outside and completed building his pile of toast. The pile was so big it was taller than Ruskin.

He went back to the drain and grasped hold of the metal cover. With all his might, he heaved it up and away from the drain hole.

He stared down into the darkness.

Down there, in the watery dark, was Krindlekrax.

And soon, Krindlekrax would smell the toast and rise from the depths to confront Ruskin.

"Come on," said Ruskin, "I'm ready for you."

His torch shone into the hole, illuminating the ladder leading down, and the water below.

Ruskin put his ear to the ground.

No rumbling.

Nothing.

Ruskin waited a little longer, then picked up a slice of toast and dropped it into the hole.

He heard it splash.

He waited.

Nothing.

He leant over the hole.

Still no rumbling.

Nothing.

Ruskin looked round him.

He imagined all his neighbours curled up in their beds, sheets and blankets holding them in tightly, clocks ticking beside them, eyes rolling behind eyelids as they dreamed, unaware that he – Ruskin Splinter – was poised over a drain, waiting to do battle with Krindlekrax.

And what would they be dreaming?

Mr and Mrs Cave would be dreaming of their pub with its stained-wood bar and satin cushions and carpet with magnolias on.

Mrs Walnut would be dreaming of the day she could close the grocer's shop once and for all and stop smelling of potatoes.

Mr Flick would be dreaming of his black velvet lapels and all the films he'd yet to show.

Mr Lace would be dreaming of pencils and Shakespeare.

Dr Flowers would be dreaming of the day he would stop sneezing.

Elvis would be dreaming of smashing all the windows in the world.

Sparkey would be dreaming of saying "Yes, sir" to everything for the rest of his life.

And in his house, his own Mum and Dad were busily dreaming too. Wendy of toast and tea and saying, "Polly-wolly-doodle-all-the-day", and his Dad of elephants and tigers and how happy he had felt in his zoo-keeper's uniform.

Ruskin was in the midst of these thoughts when . . .

"Eeeek!" went a noise.

Ruskin jumped.

He dropped the walking stick. It disappeared into the hole and landed with a splash in the water below.

"Eeeek!" went the noise again.

It was only the pub sign, but in Ruskin's nervous state it had scared him. And now Corky's walking stick was in the sewer.

Ruskin stared into the hole.

He'd already lost the medal. He couldn't lose the walking stick as well.

Ruskin took a deep breath.

There was no alternative.

He would have to go into the sewer.

He swung his legs over the edge and started climbing down the ladder.

The last sound he heard before he disappeared beneath Lizard Street was the pub sign, still going "Eeeek".

13

When Ruskin got to the bottom of the ladder he stood on a brick ledge and stared at the sewer water running alongside like a dark green river.

There were tin cans in the water and bits of paper and carrots and bananas, and all kinds of things Ruskin couldn't distinguish. His torchlight shone over walls covered with slime so thick it looked like grass.

When he glanced up, Ruskin saw a circle of stars sparkling in the drain hole above.

He looked round, searching for the walking stick.

I've got to find it, he thought.

He started to walk along the brick ledge, being careful not to slip.

It was cold in the sewer and full of echoing sounds that made his ear-drums ring.

Suddenly, Ruskin saw the walking stick.

It was floating in the water.

The current was carrying it along, deeper and deeper into the heart of the sewers.

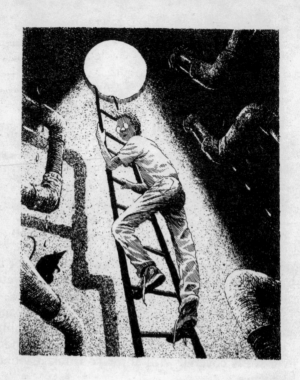

Ruskin ran until he was alongside the stick, then got to his knees and reached out.

He stretched as far as he could.

His fingers just touched the walking stick, when the current carried it off again.

Ruskin jumped up and followed.

He was breathing very hard now and – despite being cold – was sweating.

The torchlight flickered over walls and across the water.

Corky was right, Ruskin thought. It *is* beautiful down here.

The green of the slime sparkled like emeralds and the water was satin smooth.

The walking stick stopped moving.

It had got attached to some particularly thick slime.

Ruskin rushed up, got to his knees and reached out.

His fingertips grazed across the surface of the water.

He grabbed hold of the walking stick.

"Got it!" he said.

And that's when he realised. It wasn't slime the stick was attached to.

It was rats.

14

Ruskin screamed.

The water was alive with rats. Fat, dark rats, with red eyes and long pink tails, and feet like vicious claws.

The rats swam in the water and, as they swam, so they carried the walking stick with them.

Ruskin followed.

Deeper and deeper into the sewer.

He had never been this alone before. He'd always been in the bustle of Lizard Street and – even when Elvis and Sparkey stopped being his friends and he thought he was alone, he wasn't really – he'd always had Mr and Mrs Cave and Mrs Walnut and Mr Flick and Mr Lace and Dr Flowers and his Mum and Dad and, of course, Corky.

But now . . .

Now, there was no one.

Just darkness and water and hundreds of rats carrying the walking stick farther and farther into the labyrinth of darkness.

Perhaps I'll never find my way out, Ruskin thought. Perhaps I'll have to stay here for ever.

Suddenly, the rats climbed out of the water and, one at a time, disappeared into a rat-hole in the brick ledge.

The rats tried to take the walking stick with them, but the curve of the handle was too big to go through.

When all the rats had gone into the hole, Ruskin rushed up and grabbed hold of the stick.

He pulled.

It was stuck!

He pulled harder.

Still stuck!

I haven't come all this way to give up now, he thought.

He pulled again.

Still stuck.

Ruskin stood up straight, took a deep breath, then spat on his hands and rubbed them together.

He grabbed hold of the walking stick.

"This one's for Corky," he said.

And pulled as hard as he could.

"Squelch!" went the walking stick, coming out of the hole.

But the force of Ruskin's tug was so strong that, still grabbing the stick, he toppled and fell backwards into the water.

Slimy green water went up his nose and into his ears.

Ruskin coughed and spluttered.

Fortunately, the water wasn't that deep and only came up to Ruskin's knees.

He stood there for a while, clutching the walking stick.

And then he thought of something.

I must smell of toast, Ruskin thought. So why hasn't Krindlekrax come after me? Perhaps Krindlekrax doesn't exist. Perhaps it was just a story, after all. Just like his Mum had said. Nothing but a story.

He couldn't help feeling relieved at the thought of it.

Ruskin started to laugh and splash about in the water.

"A story!" he cried. And his voice echoed round him. "A story . . . story . . . story . . . story . . . story . . . ory . . . y . . ."

And he called again. Louder this time.

"STORY! STORY! STORY! STORY! Story! . . . ory . . . ory . . . y . . . y . . . y . . .

But this time his echoes were interrupted by another sound.

A roar like a million car brakes screeching all at once.

"RAAAAAHHHHH!"

Ruskin froze.

He heard the sound of splashing getting closer.

Waves appeared in the water.

"RAAAAAAHHHHHH!" went the roar again.

Ruskin started to run.

The roars got louder and louder.

It was Kindlekrax!

"RAAAAAAAHHHHHHH!"

He could feel hot air on the back of his neck.

"RAAAAAAAAHHHHHHHH!"

Ruskin reached the ladder and started to climb.

His feet slipped on the rungs a few times, but he still managed to get to the surface.

He ran down Lizard Street and hid behind the pile of toast.

He stared at the hole in the road.

Don't be scared, Ruskin thought. This is what I wanted to happen. This is what I hoped for. To come face to face with the monster. This is the only way. I should be pleased.

He clutched the walking stick as tightly as he could.

Be brave, he thought.

Suddenly, mustering all his courage, he jumped on top of the pile of toast and, waving the walking stick in the air, cried, "I'm ready for you, monster!"

That's when Krindlekrax appeared.

15

A claw.

A gleaming, black, sharp claw.

Then another claw.

And another . . .

Until a whole leg came to the surface.

A dark, green, scaly leg, dripping with slime.

Then another claw.

A gleaming, black, sharp claw.

Then another.

Until a second, dark, green, scaly leg came to the surface.

Ruskin was so scared he couldn't move. He felt as if his feet were stuck to the toast. He wondered if the congealed butter had hardened round the soles of his boots, trapping him. Then he realised he couldn't move his knees either, or his arms, or his neck, or even his eyes.

His eyes were wide open and staring at the head of Krindlekrax as it rose from the drain.

Its mouth was wider than an open car bonnet and full of sharp teeth, each one the size of a new pencil. The teeth had once been white and healthy, but now they were rotten and discoloured, with slime trickling between the gums. Its breath was hot and smelt of toast and there were flies buzzing round its tongue and nostrils. Its eyes were red, as bright as traffic lights, and its nostrils flared and leaked green liquid.

More of Krindlekrax climbed out of the drain.

Its belly was fat and dark, its back legs as claw-sharp as the front, its tail long and pointed. It was the biggest thing Ruskin had ever seen.

Ruskin thought, it could swallow me whole.

And he wished he was back in bed, tucked up and safe, his lips sticky and warm with marmalade and tea.

Krindlekrax started to sniff the toast.

"Clack!" went the jaws.

It munched the toast for a while, then swallowed and took another step forward.

"Sniff!"

"Clack!"

"Munch!"

Step forward.

Ruskin thought, I must move. I must do something.

"Sniff!"

"Clack!"

"Munch!"

Step forward.

Ruskin could feel Krindlekrax's hot breath against his cheek.

"Sniff!"

"Clack!"

"Munch!"

Step forward.

DO SOMETHING! Ruskin thought.

"Sniff . . ."

Krindlekrax was sniffing the pile of toast.

Its jaws opened wide.

Ruskin stared into the pink, steaming cave of its mouth.

In a moment the jaws will clack on me, thought Ruskin.

And then . . .

"Da-boing!"

No, Ruskin thought. It can't be!

"Da-boing! Da-boing!"

Krindlekrax stared over Ruskin's shoulder.

Ruskin didn't have to look behind him to know what was there. He knew that, at the other end of Lizard Street, a sleep-walking Elvis had left the pub and was dreamily bouncing his football.

Krindlekrax lost interest in both the pile of toast and Ruskin. Slowly, it walked past Ruskin and started to approach Elvis.

It's going to get him, thought Ruskin. I've got to move. I've got to save Elvis.

"Da-boing!"

Suddenly, Ruskin spun round and raised the walking stick into the air.

"Oh, you terrible monster!" cried Ruskin.

Krindlekrax stopped.

Ruskin jumped from the pile of toast, ran down the street and leaped on to Krindlekrax's tail.

Krindlekrax roared.

"RAAAAHHHH!"

Ruskin ran up the back of Krindlekrax – treading carefully so as not to slip on the slime – until he

was standing on Krindlekrax's head. It was very
high and Ruskin felt a little giddy. But he didn't let
this stop him. He was determined now. He knew
he had to tame Krindlekrax and protect – not only
Elvis – but the whole of Lizard Street.

"I am brave and wise and wonderful . . ." cried Ruskin, striking the top of Krindlekrax's head with the walking stick.

Krindlekrax roared again and tried to flick Ruskin from its head, as if Ruskin was nothing more than an irritating fly.

Ruskin got to his knees, then sat astride the neck of the giant crocodile.

". . . and handsome and tall . . ." continued Ruskin, "and covered in muscles, with a voice like thunder."

Krindlekrax continued to try to shake Ruskin off. But Ruskin's legs only gripped the scaly skin tighter.

"You can shake your head all you like," Ruskin said, "but it won't get me off."

Then Krindlekrax's tail curled round and hit Elvis.

Elvis fell to the ground, the ball rolling into the gutter.

Something else rolled as well.

Something gold and shining.

It was Corky's medal.

Krindlekrax saw the golden medal and stopped shaking.

It sniffed the medal.

Ruskin jumped off Krindlekrax's back and rushed over to Elvis.

"Oh, please wake up," pleaded Ruskin, shaking Elvis. "You've got to go to bed. It's not safe out here tonight."

But Elvis continued to sleep, snoring slightly, and reaching out for the ball.

Elvis found the ball and gripped it tightly. He got to his feet and started to bounce it.

"Da-boing! Da-boing!"

Krindlekrax heard the bouncing and, losing interest in the medal, roared at Ruskin and Elvis.

What can I do? thought Ruskin, panicking now. There must be a way to tame the monster. I just don't know what it is.

And then Ruskin heard something.

"Eeeek" went the noise.

It was the pub sign.

Ruskin looked up and, as he did so, the torch on his helmet illuminated the baby crocodile with a penny in its mouth.

If only I had a golden penny, thought Ruskin.

BUT I DO HAVE ONE!

The medal! Of course! Corky's golden medal!

Immediately Ruskin reached out, grabbed hold of the medal and hurled it into the crocodile's mouth.

The medal stuck at the back of Krindlekrax's throat.

Krindlekrax closed its jaws and stared at Ruskin.

It didn't move.

Ruskin got to his feet.

It had started to rain now and there was the sound of distant thunder. Raindrops landed in Krindlekrax's eyes, giving the impression of tears.

Although, of course, the medal was very small in Krindlekrax's throat, it was obviously causing a lot of discomfort.

Krindlekrax started to cough, trying to dislodge it.

Ruskin stood in front of Krindlekrax and tapped it on the nose with his walking stick.

"Don't you like the medal in your throat?" asked Ruskin.

Krindlekrax just stared.

"Open your mouth," Ruskin said. "Open your mouth and I will take the medal away."

Slowly, Krindlekrax opened its mouth.

"But," continued Ruskin, "if I do this, you must never come to Lizard Street again."

Krindlekrax's mouth remained open.

Ruskin stepped over the bottom row of Krindlekrax's teeth, and crawled into the soft, pink mouth.

It was like entering a cave full of steam, like when Wendy left the kettle boiling and the kitchen got hot and damp.

Slime dripped from the roof of the mouth and trickled down Ruskin's neck. The slime was thick and very sticky, like marmalade.

Despite the sticky slime and the slippery tongue, Ruskin found it oddly comforting in the mouth of Krindlekrax. It smelt of toast and reminded him of home.

Ruskin dislodged the medal from Krindlekrax's

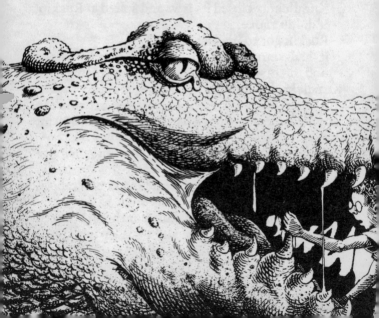

throat and crawled back out of the mouth, clutching the medal in his hands.

"Now go back to the sewer for ever!" exclaimed Ruskin. "Lizard Street is full of my friends and I don't want you here."

Slowly, Krindlekrax turned round and started to walk back down Lizard Street towards the drain.

Ruskin watched it go, saying, "Mr Lace is my friend because he gave me coloured pencils."

Krindlekrax started to climb down the drain.

Its head disappeared.

Ruskin said, "Mrs Walnut is my friend because she gave me chocolate biscuits."

The front legs of Krindlekrax disappeared.

"Dr Flowers is my friend," said Ruskin, "because he gave me a handkerchief."

The belly of Krindlekrax disappeared.

"Mr Flick is my friend," said Ruskin, "because he gave me a photograph."

The back legs of Krindlekrax disappeared.

"Mr and Mrs Cave are my friends," said Ruskin, "because they gave me some cherryade."

The tail of Krindlekrax disappeared.

The street was empty except for Ruskin and Elvis.

Ruskin looked at Elvis.

"And you are my friend," Ruskin said. "Even if you don't want to be."

There was a crack of thunder and lightning, and the rain suddenly poured down.

It felt cool and refreshing and Ruskin stared up at the sky and let the rain splash over his face.

"And Sparkey is my friend," said Ruskin, rain bubbling between his lips. "Even if he doesn't want to be."

Then Ruskin looked at the pub sign.

"Eeeek" went the sign.

"And Corky is my friend," said Ruskin. "Even if he's not here any more."

And, as Ruskin said this, so the rain washed away the peeling paint of the sign, erasing the baby crocodile.

Ruskin glanced at Elvis.

"You can stay out in the rain," he said. "I'm going to bed."

Ruskin put the drain-cover back on the drain, then went into his house and up to his bedroom.

He got into bed and closed his eyes.

The last thing he heard before he fell asleep was Elvis trying to bounce his football in the rain.

"Da-splash-boing!"

"Da-splash-boing!"

"Da-splash-boing!"

16

"Wake up!"

Ruskin opened his eyes to see Wendy standing beside his bed with a plate of toast and a cup of tea.

"I've been trying to wake you for ages," Wendy said, putting the tea and toast on Ruskin's bedside table. "How are you feeling?"

"Fine, thank you," replied Ruskin, eating the toast.

"You're not going to stay in bed again?" his Mum asked.

"Certainly not," Ruskin said, jumping out of bed. "It's a beautiful day."

"Yes," said Wendy. "It rained during the night and it's a lot cooler now."

Ruskin sipped some tea, then said, "Besides, it's the school play today. I want to see how Elvis plays the hero. You know, Elvis is still my friend, even though he doesn't want to be."

"That's what you were saying in your sleep," Wendy said. "You were saying, Elvis is your friend

and Mr Flick is your friend and . . ."

She was interrupted by someone knocking at the front door.

"Who can that be?" asked Wendy, nervously. Then added, "Polly-wolly-doodle-all-the-day."

Winston poked his head round the bedroom door.

"We've got a visitor," he said.

"They're knocking on the door very loudly," Wendy said, nervously.

"It's not my fault," said Winston.

"Oh, stop it, you two!" cried Ruskin, pushing past them and rushing down the stairs. "Why are you so nervous about everything?"

Ruskin opened the street door and found Mr Lace on the doorstep.

"Oh, a tragedy beyond words!" exclaimed Mr Lace, running his fingers through his hair and sucking a pencil.

"What's happened?" asked Ruskin.

"Elvis was sleep-walking in the rain last night," cried Mr Lace. "He's caught a terrible cold and can't do the play any more. You're the only person who knows the lines!" Mr Lace grabbed Ruskin's hands and squeezed them tightly. "Please be the hero," he begged. "We need you."

"I'd love to," said Ruskin, casually. Then, looking back at Wendy and Winston who were hiding at the top of the stairs, called, "Get dressed you two! You're coming to school to see me do a bit of acting."

"Oh, polly-wolly . . ." began Wendy.

"Stop saying that," interrupted Ruskin, firmly.

"It's not my . . ." began Winston.

"Stop saying that," interrupted Ruskin, even more firmly. "Just get to school. I'm going to be a star."

17

The whole of Lizard Street came to St George's Main Hall to see the school play.

Ruskin and Mr Lace stood behind the makeshift stage curtain at the front of the hall and peered through a crack at the assembled crowd.

Ruskin was holding a plastic shield and sword.

"Are you nervous?" asked Mr Lace, sucking a pencil.

"No," replied Ruskin.

"Not at all?"

"No," Ruskin said. "Why should I be? I told you before. I was born to be a hero."

Mr Lace put his arm round Ruskin's shoulder and squeezed.

"I think you're right," said Mr Lace.

Beside Ruskin was the cardboard-and-chicken-wire dragon. Ruskin looked up into the red milk-bottle tops of its eyes.

"Let's do battle," he said.

Mr Lace rushed to the side of the stage and pulled

open the curtains.

A few people in the audience gasped when they saw Ruskin dressed as the hero. One or two of them were even tempted to laugh. But as soon as Ruskin spoke, all that changed.

As soon as he started his performance, everyone believed he was the hero. There was no doubt in anyone's mind. They sat there, eyes wide, mouths open, totally captivated by the magnificence of Ruskin's acting.

At the end of the play when Ruskin jumped on the back of the dragon and cried out, "Oh, you terrible monster. You scary thing of the dark. You will scare us no more. I am not afraid. I have tamed you and now I am your master," people in the audience clapped and cheered.

When the play was over, Ruskin was given a standing ovation.

Mr Lace lifted Ruskin into the air and cried, "A hero!"

Everyone patted Ruskin on the back and said how wonderful he was.

People came up to Wendy and Winston and spoke to them.

"Your son is such a good actor," said Mrs Walnut. "I don't think anyone could have done it better."

"Certainly not," agreed Mr Flick. "He's our little star."

"A star absolutely," said Dr Flowers. "I never knew he . . . TISHOO! . . . had it in him."

Even Mr and Mrs Cave came over and remarked how good Ruskin was.

"You must come to the pub and have a chat," said Mr Cave, putting his arm round Winston's shoulders. "We don't see enough of you."

Mrs Cave said, "You must be proud of your son."

"We are," said Wendy. "He wants to be an actor and act in plays by Shakespeare."

"Oh, don't say that name!" cried Mr Lace, tears springing to his eyes.

Everyone laughed and vowed they would try not to say "Shakespeare" in the presence of Mr Lace again.

Ruskin watched everyone talking and laughing and having a good time.

"Ruskin," said a voice.

Ruskin turned to see Sparkey Walnut standing beside him. Sparkey looked very bashful and shuffled from side to side.

"Hello, Sparkey," Ruskin said. "How have you been?"

"Very well," replied Sparkey, staring at the floor.

"I'm glad you're out of bed."

"Yes," said Ruskin. "I felt very ill for a while, but everything's all right now."

"You're acting was very good," remarked Sparkey. "I was so excited when you were fighting the monster. I cheered and clapped along with all the others."

"Thank you," said Ruskin.

"Do you think . . ." began Sparkey, and then his voice broke off and he looked away.

"Say it," said Ruskin.

"Do you think we could be friends again?" asked Sparkey.

"We never stopped being friends," said Ruskin.

Suddenly everyone in the hall heard a noise.

"Da-boing!"

"Smash!"

"Da-boing!"

"SMAAAAASH!"

People stopped talking and looked out of the window.

Elvis was in Lizard Street. He was smashing every window in sight and screaming, "I wanted to be the hero! I wanted to be the hero!"

Ruskin stamped his foot.

"I'm going to stop this smashing once and for all," Ruskin said.

Ruskin marched out of the hall, down the stairs, across the playground and into Lizard Street.

Wendy and Winston and all the other people of Lizard Street stayed in the hall. They knew how dangerous Elvis could be when he was in one of his window-smashing moods.

Ruskin marched up to Elvis.

Elvis was wearing his pyjamas with the padded shoulders and his helmet with a visor. His nose was very red because of his cold and he smelt of medicine.

"You!" cried Elvis, pointing at Ruskin. "You stole my part! You take everything from me." And he bounced the ball.

"Da-boing!"

It smashed Mr Lace's window, landed in his living room, bounced out through another window, and landed in Elvis's hands.

"There's not going to be any glass left in Lizard Street by the time I'm finished," growled Elvis. "I'm going to break Mr Lace's windows and Mrs Walnut's windows and . . ."

"No you're not," said Ruskin, calmly.

Elvis glared at him. "You silly little Splinter," he growled. "You can't stop me. I'm big and you're small. I've got muscles and you've got none. My voice is deep like thunder and yours is . . ."

"Oh, be quiet," said Ruskin. "I'm fed up with you. You're so . . . so wild. Too much wildness is boring. I'm going to tame you and make you interesting again."

And, with that, Ruskin snatched the ball from Elvis's hands.

The people of Lizard Street – who were still watching from the school-hall window – gasped.

Ruskin took the pin that had been attached to Corky's medal from his pocket, raised it in the air, then stuck it into the ball.

Air gushed from the puncture. The ball whizzed out of Ruskin's hands and flew around Lizard Street in circles.

It whizzed up into the air.

Whizzed past the people at the school-hall window.

Past the pub.

Past Mrs Walnut's shop.

Past Dr Flowers's house.

Past Mr Flick's cinema.

Past Corky's old house.

Past Mr Lace's house.

Then it hovered in front of Ruskin's house for a while, before falling into the drain and out of sight.

The people at the window cheered.

Elvis stared at the drain.

He listened to the people of Lizard Street cheering.

Then he looked at Ruskin. "No one likes me," he said.

Then he fell to his knees and started to cry.

"I . . . I never wanted to grow this tall," said Elvis.

"I hate it. Why did it have to happen? All I wanted was to stay small like you and Sparkey. Why did things have to change? I don't want these muscles, I don't want a voice like thunder. I want to play on the swings and eat lots of ice-cream and . . . and have people tell me how cute I am. But they don't. They . . . they think I'm grown up. But . . . but I'm not. And I don't want to be."

Elvis was crying so much he could barely speak now. "And I wanted to be friends with Corky. But he liked you . . . more than he liked me . . . and he . . . he bought you a ball . . . He bought it for you because you were small. And I got . . . nothing . . . nothing . . ."

"That's why you stole the ball," said Ruskin.

"Yes," Elvis said. "I was so jealous. I'm . . . I'm sorry, Ruskin."

The people of Lizard Street had left the school by now and were standing around Ruskin.

They all stared at Elvis.

"I miss Corky," said Elvis, still crying. "I miss hearing his broom sweep the playground."

Ruskin helped Elvis to his feet.

"We all miss him," said Ruskin. "But we don't have to break glass."

"Can we be friends again?" asked Elvis.

"We always have been," replied Ruskin.

Elvis and Ruskin hugged each other.

The people of Lizard Street cheered.

Ruskin looked at them and said, "I used to think that Lizard Street was the cracked pavement and the dark brick and the road with holes in. But it's not! Lizard Street is me, and my Mum and Dad, and Elvis, and Sparkey, and Dr Flowers, and Mr Lace, and Mr Flick, and Mrs Walnut, and Mr and Mrs

Cave, and — even though he's not here — Corky Pigeon." And then, in the loudest voice he could muster, he cried, "I LOVE YOU, LIZARD STREET! I LOVE YOU! I LOVE YOU! I LOVE YOU!"

THE END